CURSED

Tales of the World's Most Haunted Objects

ETHAN HAYES

FREE REIGN

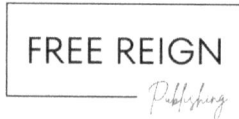

FREE REIGN
Publishing

CONTENTS

INTRODUCTION

In *Cursed: Tales of the World's Most Haunted Objects*, bestselling author Ethan Hayes takes us on a spine-tingling journey into the heart of darkness, where objects are not merely inanimate but bearers of profound, often terrifying histories. This book is not just a collection of stories; it is a labyrinth of the unexplained and the unsettling, where each artifact holds a mirror to our deepest fears and superstitions.

For centuries, tales of cursed objects have permeated our folklore and reality, blurring the lines between myth and fact. From the glittering yet ominous Hope Diamond to the eerie whispers surrounding the Dybbuk Box, these objects captivate our imagination and challenge our understanding of the natural world. Hayes, with his characteristic depth of research and compelling storytelling, not only recounts the histories of these famed objects but also delves into the psychological, cultural, and some-times paranormal facets that have cemented their noto-riety in human history.

What is it about these objects that continues to fasci-nate and horrify us? Is it the allure of the unknown, the thrill of touching something that bridges the gap between life and death, or the sheer magnetic pull of their often tragic and blood-stained pasts? Hayes explores these questions with a keen eye, weaving a tapestry of narratives that is as educational as it is enthralling.

Cursed is more than a book; it is an expedition into the shadows of history. It invites you, the reader, to step closer, to gaze into the abyss of the cursed and the haunted. Ethan Hayes, with his compelling prose and meticulous research, serves as your guide through a world where the past is never truly dead and where objects hold secrets far darker than their surface suggests.

Prepare to be enthralled, enlightened, and perhaps even a little terrified. Welcome to the world of *Cursed: Tales of the World's Most Haunted Objects.*

CHAPTER 1

KING TUTANKHAMUN'S TOMB (CURSE OF THE PHARAOHS)

The legend of the "Curse of the Pharaohs" associated with King Tutankhamun's tomb is steeped in mystery and has captured the public's imagination for decades. This story finds its roots in the events following the opening of Tutankhamun's tomb in 1923 by archaeologist Howard Carter and his financier, Lord Carnarvon.

The death of Lord Carnarvon, merely two months after the tomb's opening, served as the catalyst for the curse's legend. Carnarvon's demise was attributed to blood poisoning from a mosquito bite, but the timing of his death following the tomb's opening led to widespread speculation and fear of a mummy's curse. The media played a significant role in fueling these speculations. Sir Arthur Conan Doyle, the famous creator of Sherlock Holmes, publicly stated his belief that Carnarvon had

Howard Carter

fallen victim to the "Pharaoh's Curse."

Lord Carnarvon

The press at the time was rife with stories that embell-ished the idea of the curse. For instance, they reported on a supposed curse inscription found in the tomb, warning of death to those who disturbed the king's rest. Although no such inscription was recorded by the excavating Egyptolo-gists, the story captured the public's imagination.

Additionally, the media reported various mysterious incidents purportedly linked to the curse. One such inci-dent involved the death of Carnarvon's dog back in

England at the exact moment of his owner's passing. There were also reports of a power outage in Cairo at the time of Carnarvon's death, adding to the eerie circumstances surrounding the event.

The fascination with the curse persisted over the years. During the 1970s, when some of Tutankhamun's treasures went on a world tour, there was apprehension among the public about the potential reach of the curse. This included an incident where a policeman guarding Tutankhamun's funerary mask in San Francisco claimed that the curse caused him a mild stroke.

While serious Egyptologists and historians generally regard the curse as a myth, its legacy in popular culture is undeniable. The tale of the "Curse of King Tutankhamun's Tomb" not only highlights the allure of ancient Egypt but also underscores the human fascination with the mysterious and the unexplained.

CHAPTER 2

ANNABELLE THE DOLL

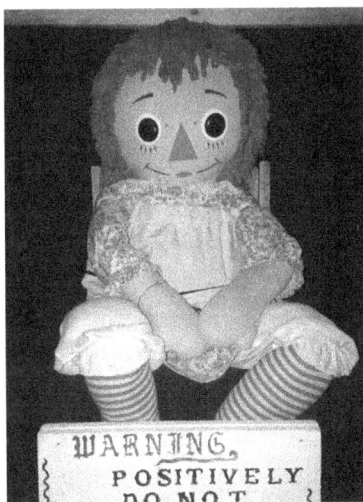

Annabelle in the Warren's, Occult Museum in Monroe, Connecticut

In 1970, Donna, a nursing student, received a Raggedy Ann doll from her mother as a birthday gift. The doll was purchased from a hobby store, a seemingly innocent gift to brighten her apartment. Donna and her roommate, Angie, soon noticed peculiar activities surrounding the doll. The doll appeared to change positions on its own, moving from one room to another without any logical explanation.

The unsettling occurrences escalated when the doll started leaving handwritten notes saying "Help me." These notes were written on parchment paper, a type Donna and Angie did not keep in their apartment. One night, Donna came home to find the doll in a different room with what appeared to be blood on its hands and chest. These incidents prompted the roommates to seek help from a medium.

During a séance, the medium informed Donna and Angie that the doll was inhabited by the spirit of a young girl named Annabelle Higgins. According to the medium, Annabelle was a seven-year-old girl whose lifeless body was found in a field upon which their apartment complex was built. The spirit claimed to feel comfortable and safe with Donna and Angie, asking for permission to stay with them. Moved by the story, Donna consented, allowing the spirit to inhabit the doll. However, this decision did not bring peace. Instead, the disturbances became more malevolent and frequent.

Feeling increasingly threatened, Donna and Angie contacted Ed and Lorraine Warren, renowned paranormal investigators. The Warrens quickly concluded that the doll was not possessed by the spirit of a young girl but by a malevolent demonic entity. They explained that spirits do not possess inanimate objects like dolls; instead, an inhuman spirit can attach itself to a place or object and manipulate it to create the illusion of being alive, all in an effort to possess a human host.

Lorraine Warren with Annabelle

The Warrens conducted an exorcism of the apartment to cleanse it of any residual negative energy. They then took the doll, fearing that the demonic presence might escalate its activities if left unchecked. During the car ride to their home, the Warrens experienced several near-fatal incidents, including brake failures and steering issues. These issues ceased only after Ed doused the doll with holy water.

The Warrens placed Annabelle in their Occult Museum in Monroe, Connecticut. The doll was secured in a specially made glass and wood case, upon which they inscribed the Lord's Prayer and Saint Michael's Prayer. Ed Warren would periodically recite a binding prayer over the case to ensure the spirit remained trapped.

Despite being locked away, Annabelle's legend continued to grow. Visitors to the museum often reported eerie feelings or mishaps after interacting with the doll. One priest who mocked Annabelle experienced brake failure and a near-fatal accident on his way home. Another visitor, who tapped on the glass case and laughed at the warnings, died in a motorcycle accident shortly after leaving the museum.

Annabelle's story gained widespread fame through its depiction in the "Conjuring" film universe. The movies, however, portray a fictionalized and far more sinister-looking porcelain doll, distinct from the real Raggedy Ann doll. The films, including "Annabelle" (2014), "Annabelle: Creation" (2017), and "Annabelle Comes Home" (2019), have grossed over $800 million worldwide, solidifying Annabelle's place in horror folklore.

Skeptics argue that the story of Annabelle is a fabrication, designed to enhance the Warrens' reputation and the allure of their Occult Museum. Critics point out that the evidence supporting the supernatural claims is anecdotal and primarily comes from the Warrens themselves. Science writers like Sharon A. Hill argue that the myths surrounding Annabelle and other objects in the Warrens' collection are likely self-generated, with no concrete proof to back them up.

The Occult Museum, which houses Annabelle, has been closed to the public due to zoning issues, but the doll

'Annabelle' movie poster, courtesy of Warner Bros. Pictures

remains a topic of fascination and fear. Tony Spera, the Warrens' son-in-law, who currently oversees the collection, occasionally releases updates and reassurances about the doll's containment. Despite the museum's closure, Annabelle continues to draw interest from paranormal enthusiasts and skeptics alike.

Based on the available evidence, it seems plausible that the legend of Annabelle has been exaggerated over the years. While the experiences of Donna, Angie, and Lou are unsettling, they are also subjective and lack corroborative evidence. The dramatic incidents reported by the Warrens could be interpreted as confirmation bias or the result of suggestion. Without concrete scientific proof, it is challenging to definitively conclude that the doll is haunted or cursed. The Annabelle story, whether true or not, remains a compelling narrative that blurs the line between reality and the supernatural.

CHAPTER 3
THE CRYING BOY PAINTING

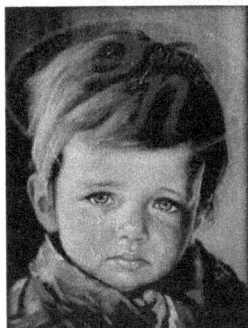

The Crying Boy paintings were created by Italian painter Giovanni Bragolin, a pseudonym for Bruno Amadio, in the 1950s. These paintings depicted young children with tear-filled eyes and sorrowful expressions. The series became surprisingly popular, with over 50,000 prints sold in the UK alone. The paintings were initially intended as souvenirs for tourists, symbolizing the war orphans of World War II.

The curse of The Crying Boy painting began to gain notoriety in 1985 when a British tabloid, The Sun, published a story about a house fire in South Yorkshire. The fire reportedly destroyed everything except a print of The Crying Boy, which was found untouched among the rubble. This incident led to a surge of similar reports from people who claimed that their homes had burned down, leaving only The Crying Boy paintings unscathed. Firefighters logged over 50 such incidents, fueling the legend that the painting was cursed.

The legend includes a story about the painting's subject, a mute orphan named Don Bonillo, who was said to bring fires wherever he went. The painter, ignoring a priest's warning, adopted the boy, only to experience a devastating fire that destroyed his studio. This event further solidified the notion of the curse, with the boy eventually dying in a fiery car crash in 1976, adding to the painting's ominous reputation.

Despite the widespread belief in the curse, there are scientific explanations that debunk the supernatural claims. Firefighters and investigators suggested that the paintings were coated with a varnish that made them fire-resistant. This varnish could explain why the paint-ings often survived fires that consumed everything else. Additionally, the lightweight nature of the prints might cause them to fall face down, protecting the image from flames.

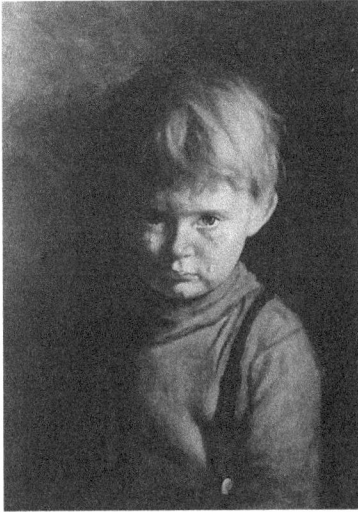

Alan Wilkinson, a fire station officer, logged numerous cases involving The Crying Boy and suggested that the cause of the fires was typically mundane, such as faulty wiring or kitchen accidents. The survival of the paintings could be attributed to their materials and placement rather than any supernatural influence.

Many homeowners shared their experiences with the cursed painting. For instance, Ron and Mary Hall from Rotherham reported that their house was gutted by fire, yet the Crying Boy print remained intact. Similar stories from other victims included reports of accidents and misfortunes after acquiring the painting, further entrenching the belief in its curse.

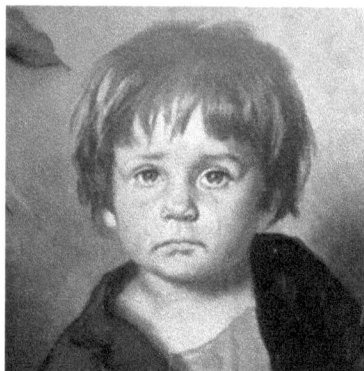

Today, the belief in the curse of The Crying Boy has waned, though it remains a popular topic in paranormal circles and urban legend discussions. The paintings are still collected and can be found in various auctions and antique shops. Some people even collect them specifically because of the legend, treating them as curious artifacts of modern folklore.

In an effort to debunk the curse, The Sun newspaper organized a mass burning of Crying Boy paintings on Halloween in 1985. Despite initial difficulties in igniting the prints, they eventually burned, dispelling some of the mystique surrounding the curse.

The Crying Boy has made its way into popular culture, featuring in ghost-hunting TV shows and YouTube videos. The legend has been discussed in various podcasts and articles, keeping the story alive in the digital age. Shows like "The UnXplained" and numerous paranormal investigation channels on YouTube have explored the myth, often with a skeptical yet entertaining approach.

While the eerie tales and numerous eyewitness accounts lend an air of mystery to The Crying Boy painting, scientific explanations and critical investigations suggest that the so-called curse is more likely a series of coincidences amplified by media sensationalism. The painting's survival in fires can be reasonably explained by its materials and physical properties rather than any supernatural cause. Thus, while The Crying Boy remains a fascinating piece of cursed art lore, the evidence leans heavily towards debunking its haunted reputation.

CHAPTER 4
GRIGORI RASPUTIN

Grigori Yefimovich Rasputin, born on January 21, 1869, in the small village of Pokrovskoye in Siberia, emerged from humble beginnings to become one of the most enigmatic and controversial figures in Russian history.

His father, Yefim Yakovlevich, was a peasant farmer and a church elder, and his mother, Anna Parshukova, bore several children, all of whom died in infancy except for Grigori.

From a young age, Rasputin exhibited an intense religious fervor and claimed to have visions. He gained a reputation for clairvoyance and healing, which set the foundation for his later influence. In 1897, he left his village to live in a monastery, where he adopted an ascetic lifestyle. This period of spiritual growth saw him traveling extensively, including to the Monastery of the Caves in Kiev and Saint Alexander Nevsky Monastery, where he mingled with influential religious figures.

Rasputin's ascent to power began in 1905 when he was introduced to Tsar Nicholas II and Tsarina Alexandra by Grand Duchess Milica of Montenegro. At this time, the royal couple was desperate for a cure for their son Alexei, who suffered from hemophilia. Rasputin's ability to seemingly alleviate Alexei's symptoms, particularly by advising against the use of aspirin— a blood thinner—cemented his place in the royal court. The Tsarina, in particular, placed immense trust in Rasputin, believing him to be divinely guided.

Rasputin's influence grew significantly during World War I when Tsar Nicholas left Petrograd to command the Russian Army. In his absence, Alexandra relied heavily on Rasputin for political and personal advice, which further fueled rumors and discontent among the nobility and the public. His enemies accused him of meddling in state affairs, and his unorthodox behavior, including alleged promiscuity and heavy drinking, tarnished his reputation.

Nicholas with his family (left to right): Olga, Maria, Nicholas II, Alexandra Fyodorovna, Anastasia, Alexei, and Tatiana. Livadia Palace, 1913.

Rasputin's life was marred by numerous controversies. He was accused of sexual misconduct, blasphemy, and heresy. His growing power and the perception of him as a corrupt influence on the monarchy led to several assassination attempts. In 1914, Chionya Guseva, a follower turned enemy, stabbed Rasputin in the abdomen, but he survived, claiming divine protection.

The final plot against Rasputin culminated on December 30, 1916. A group of nobles, including Prince

Felix Yusupov and Grand Duke Dmitri Pavlovich, invited Rasputin to Yusupov's palace, where they poisoned him with cyanide-laced cakes and wine. When the poison seemed ineffective, they shot him multiple times, and, according to legend, he continued to show signs of life until he was finally drowned in the Neva River.

Rasputin's assassination did little to stem the tide of revolution. Instead, it highlighted the deep-seated issues within the Russian Empire, contributing to the fall of the Romanov dynasty. His life and death remain shrouded in mystery, with numerous rumors and legends perpetuating his mystique. Some historians suggest that Rasputin's notoriety was amplified by propaganda and the fear he instilled in his adversaries.

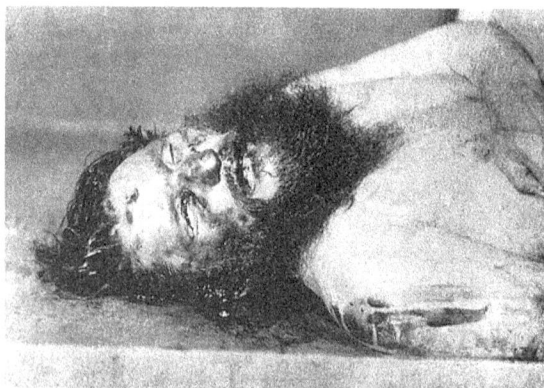

Rasputin's corpse on the ground with a bullet wound visible in his forehead

Eyewitness accounts of Rasputin's death vary, with some claiming he exhibited supernatural resilience. The involvement of key figures like Prince Yusupov adds a layer of credibility and intrigue to these stories. Yusupov himself wrote detailed accounts of the assassination, although the accuracy of his narratives has been questioned over the years.

Today, Rasputin's name is synonymous with dark mysticism and political intrigue. He has been immortalized in numerous books, films, and even songs. The fascination with his life continues, as evidenced by his portrayal in popular media, from the animated film *Anastasia* to the song *Rasputin* by Boney M. His story serves as a testament to the complex interplay between power, superstition, and historical legacy.

Rasputin's life, marked by his rise from obscurity to a figure of immense influence and his dramatic assassination, remains one of the most compelling chapters in Russian history. His legacy endures, not just as a historical figure but as a symbol of the tumultuous times that heralded the end of imperial Russia.

The Dybbuk Box, a term popularized by Kevin Mannis, refers to an antique wine cabinet claimed to be haunted by a dybbuk, a malicious spirit from Jewish folklore. The concept of a dybbuk itself stems from Jewish mysticism and folklore, where it represents a dislocated soul of a deceased person that seeks to inhabit the body of a living person, usually to resolve unfinished business or to escape punishment in the afterlife.

Kevin Mannis, an antiques dealer, purchased the box from an estate sale in Portland, Oregon, in 2003. He then crafted a backstory for the box, claiming it belonged to a Holocaust survivor who said it contained a dybbuk. According to Mannis' tale, subsequent owners of the box experienced a series of unfortunate events and paranormal phenomena, which he detailed in an eBay listing. This narrative captured the public's imagination, and the Dybbuk Box quickly became a sensational urban legend.

Skeptics argue that the story of the Dybbuk Box is a product of creative storytelling and the power of suggestion. Kevin Mannis himself admitted in 2021 that the entire story was a fabrication, crafted as a creative writing experiment. Despite this revelation, the legend of the Dybbuk Box persists, fueled by psychological factors and the cultural fascination with haunted objects.

Chris French, head of the Anomalistic Psychology Research Unit at Goldsmiths, University of London, explains that people who believe they are cursed are more likely to attribute any negative experiences to the perceived curse. This phenomenon, known as confirmation bias, reinforces their belief in the curse's power. Additionally, there is no scientific evidence to support the existence of dybbuks or their ability to inhabit inanimate objects like a box.

Various owners of the Dybbuk Box have reported eerie experiences. Mannis described nightmarish visions, mysterious smells, and disturbing events. Jason Haxton, a subsequent owner and director of the Museum of Osteopathic Medicine in Missouri, claimed to have suffered from health issues and terrifying dreams after acquiring the box. He eventually placed the box in a gold-lined wooden container, which he believed mitigated its effects.

Paranormal investigator Zak Bagans, who owns the box now and displays it in his Haunted Museum in Las Vegas, also reported strange occurrences, including experiencing a heart attack which he attributed to the box's influence. Rapper Post Malone, who visited Bagans' museum and touched the box, later blamed a series of unfortunate events on his encounter with it.

The Dybbuk Box is currently housed in Zak Bagans' Haunted Museum in Las Vegas, where it continues to attract visitors and fuel stories of supernatural phenomena. Its reputation as a cursed object remains strong, bolstered by its portrayal in popular culture and paranormal investigations.

The Dybbuk Box gained widespread attention through its depiction in the 2012 horror film "The Possession," produced by Sam Raimi. The film dramatizes the story of a young girl possessed by a spirit released from a mysterious box, loosely based on the legends surrounding the Dybbuk Box. The box has also been featured in various paranormal documentaries and television shows, further cementing its place in contemporary folklore.

The enduring fascination with the Dybbuk Box highlights the human tendency to seek out and believe in the supernatural. While the stories and experiences associated with the box are compelling, the lack of scientific evidence and .the creator's admission of fabrication strongly suggest that the Dybbuk Box is not truly haunted or cursed. Instead, it serves as a powerful example of how folklore and psychological factors can create and sustain legends.

The Dybbuk Box is a fascinating artifact of modern myth-making, blending elements of Jewish folklore with contemporary storytelling. Whether one believes in its supernatural properties or views it as a cleverly constructed hoax, the Dybbuk Box remains a compelling topic for exploration and discussion.

For further reading and detailed exploration of the Dybbuk Box's history and cultural impact, refer to the sources used for this chapter: Wikipedia, US Ghost Adventures, All That's Interesting, and Mysterious Tales.

CHAPTER 6

THE HOPE DIAMOND

The Hope Diamond, renowned for its stunning beauty and shrouded in a veil of mystery, has a history as captivating as its appearance. This legendary gemstone's journey spans continents and centuries, entwining with tales of misfortune and intrigue.

The Hope Diamond, weighing 45.52 carats and pear-shaped, exhibits a striking fancy dark grayish-blue color. It is particularly renowned for its intense red phosphorescence under ultraviolet light, a quality that has fueled its reputation as a "cursed" gemstone. The stone's chemical composition includes trace amounts of boron, which imparts its blue color.

Its story begins in India, where it was presumably mined from the Kollur mine in Guntur, part of the Golconda kingdom. French gem merchant Jean-Baptiste Tavernier acquired the gem, then known as the Tavernier Blue, during one of his voyages to India between 1640 and 1667. It's believed that he sold this and other diamonds to King Louis XIV of France around 1669.

King Louis XIV

Under King Louis XIV, the diamond was recut into the French Blue and became part of the French Crown Jewels. It remained in royal possession until the tumultuous times of the French Revolution. During this period, the French Royal family, including Louis XVI and Marie Antoinette, faced severe economic and political challenges, culminating in their execution in 1793. However, it's highly unlikely that Marie Antoinette or other members of the French Royal family ever wore the French Blue, as it was set within the Order of the Golden Fleece, serving more as a symbol of power than a piece of jewelry.

In 1792, amid the chaos of the French Revolution, the French Crown Jewels, including the French Blue, were stolen from the Garde-Meuble, the Royal Storehouse. The theft was a significant event, with the French Blue disappearing from public knowledge for several decades.

The diamond resurfaced in London around 1812, significantly recut to its current form, now known as the Hope Diamond. The first known reference to this recut diamond was by a London jeweler, John Francillon, who made a sketch and description in 1812. The recutting was likely an attempt to disguise its notorious origin as the French Blue.

❧❧❧

THE CURSE

The Hope Diamond, known for its magnificent beauty, is also infamous for its alleged curse that has fascinated and terrified many over the centuries. The legend of the curse has several notable accounts, adding a layer of mystique to its already intriguing history.

The curse is said to have originated when Jean-Baptiste Tavernier, a 17th-century French merchant, purportedly stole the diamond from a Hindu statue in India.

Jean-Baptiste Tavernier

The priests of the temple allegedly cursed the diamond and its future owners. However, reports about

Tavernier's fate vary, with some suggesting he died a painful death, while others indicate he lived to a ripe old age.

Several prominent figures throughout history have been linked to the diamond and its curse:

۞

-King Louis **XIV**:

After purchasing the diamond from Tavernier and having it recut, King Louis XIV suffered from numerous health issues and eventually died of gangrene. Interestingly, most of his legitimate children also died in childhood.

-Nicholas **Fouquet**:

A minister under King Louis XIV, Fouquet wore the diamond once.

He subsequently fell out of favor with the king, leading to his imprisonment.

Nicholas Fouquet

. . .

Louis XVI and Marie Antoinette

-LOUIS XVI AND MARIE ANTOINETTE: The diamond was inherited by Louis XVI and his wife, Marie Antoinette.

Both were executed during the French Revolution, adding to the lore of the curse.

-MARIE-LOUISE, PRINCESS DE LAMBALLE:

Léon Maxime Faivre, Death of the Princess de Lamballe, Paris, September 3, 1792. *1908, oil on canvas.*

A close friend of Marie Antoinette and a member of

her court, she wore the diamond and met a tragic end at the hands of a mob during the French Revolution.

-WILHELM FALS:

A Dutch jeweler who recut the diamond, Fals was reportedly murdered by his own son, who then took his life.

-SIMON MAONCHARIDES: A GREEK MERCHANT WHO owned the diamond, he tragically drove his car over a cliff, killing himself and his family.

-EVALYN WALSH MCLEAN: AN AMERICAN SOCIALITE who bought the diamond, McLean faced numerous personal tragedies including the deaths of her son and daughter, the infidelity and eventual mental breakdown of her husband, leading to her own financial ruin.

-JAMES TODD: THE MAILMAN WHO DELIVERED THE diamond to the Smithsonian Museum supposedly suffered a crushed leg in a truck accident, a head injury in a separate incident, and the burning down of his house.

Despite these tales, many skeptics argue that the curse is more myth than reality, a product of human fascination with curses and coincidence. The diamond, now housed in the Smithsonian Museum, continues to draw interest not only for its physical beauty but also for its storied past.

CHAPTER 7

THE ISLAND OF THE DOLLS (ISLA DE LAS MUÑECAS)

The Island of the Dolls, or Isla de las Muñecas, is located in the canals of Xochimilco, near Mexico City. The eerie legend begins with Don Julian Santana Barrera, a reclusive man who moved to the island in the mid-20th century. According to local lore, Don Julian discovered the body of a young girl who had drowned in the canal.

Haunted by the tragedy, he believed her spirit lingered on the island and began hanging dolls he found in the canal to appease her restless spirit.

Despite skepticism from his family and others who doubted the story of the drowned girl, Don Julian persisted, collecting and hanging dolls for the remainder of his life. He claimed the dolls protected him and continued to adorn the island with them until his death in 2001. Intriguingly, Don Julian was found dead in the same spot where he claimed to have discovered the girl's body.

Visitors and locals alike have reported various super-natural occurrences on the island. Many claim the dolls move their heads, arms, or open their eyes. Some have even reported hearing whispers and strange voices, adding to the island's haunted reputation.

Photographer Cindy Vasko described the island as the "creepiest place" she had ever been, noting the unsettling sight of hundreds of dolls hanging from trees and fences. Other visitors have shared similar spine-chilling experiences, reinforcing the island's eerie allure.

From a scientific standpoint, the paranormal claims associated with Isla de las Muñecas can be attributed to psychological factors. The island's isolated and macabre environment, coupled with the legend, can heighten visitors' suggestibility and perception of supernatural activity. Auditory pareidolia, a phenomenon where the brain interprets random sounds as voices, could explain the whispers heard by visitors.

Moreover, the dolls' weathered and decaying appearances can naturally create the illusion of movement, especially in the dim light and shifting shadows of the island. While these explanations provide logical reasons for the reported phenomena, they do little to diminish the island's haunting reputation.

Today, Isla de las Muñecas is a popular tourist destination. Visitors often bring their own dolls to add to the collection, continuing Don Julian's tradition. The island features a small museum displaying articles about its history and its former owner, as well as Don Julian's first and favorite doll, Agustinita.

Tourists can reach the island via a boat ride through the Xochimilco canals, a journey that showcases the region's ecological beauty before delivering them to the island's eerie landscape.

The Island of the Dolls has captured the imagination of many, making appearances in various media. It has been featured on the Travel Channel's *Ghost Adventures*, Amazon Prime's *Lore*, and *BuzzFeed Unsolved*. These shows delve into the island's haunted history, attracting paranormal enthusiasts and skeptics alike.

In literature, the island has inspired numerous works, including the poetry of Sandra Cisneros and stories by other authors fascinated by its dark legend. The island has even influenced art, with renowned Mexican artist Frida Kahlo incorporating elements of its eerie aesthetic into her paintings.

Isla de las Muñecas has become a symbol of Mexican folklore, its legend deeply ingrained in the local culture. For many, the island is not just a tourist attraction but a place of mystery and superstition, believed to harbor restless spirits. The dolls are viewed as both protectors and harbingers of curses, creating a unique blend of fear and reverence.

Whether seen as a haunted place or a curious oddity, it continues to draw visitors from around the world, each seeking to experience its unsettling charm firsthand.

CHAPTER 8
THE ICEMAN (ÖTZI)

Reconstruction of what Ötzi must have looked like

In September 1991, German tourists Helmut and Erika Simon were hiking in the Ötztal Alps, straddling the border between Austria and Italy, when they stumbled upon a remarkable find. What they initially thought was a modern mountaineer's body turned out to be one of the most significant archaeological discoveries of the century: the naturally mummified remains of a man who lived over 5,300 years ago. This ancient human, later named Ötzi after the region in which he was found, has since offered unparalleled insights into the life and times of Copper Age Europeans.

Reinhold Messner (right) looking at Ötzi after more ice had melted or been hacked away. Notice the wooden stick in his companion's right hand. It was used during the first attempts to hack Ötzi out of the ice. It is in fact part of the frame for Ötzi's backpack. In the upper right corner, we can see Ötzi's bow resting against the rock.

Ötzi's body was preserved remarkably well due to the unique climatic conditions of the high Alps. Scientists concluded that he had been swiftly covered by snow and ice shortly after his death, which shielded his remains from decomposition. Initially, it was believed that Ötzi's body had been undisturbed since his death, but recent studies suggest that his remains were periodically exposed due to shifting ice and seasonal thawing and refreezing.

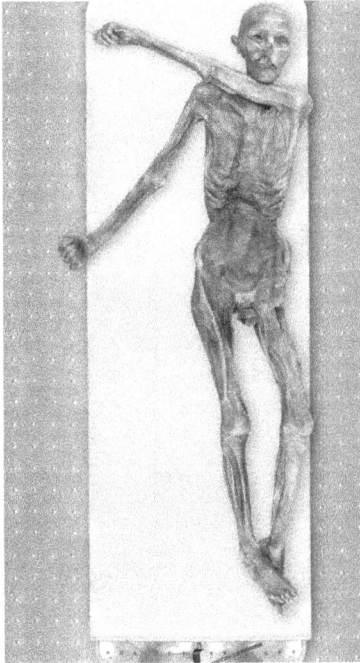

Ötzi's discovery has provided a treasure trove of information about prehistoric life. Analysis of his body and the artifacts found with him have revealed a detailed picture of his last days. He carried a copper axe, a symbol of status and advanced metallurgy for his time, alongside flint tools, a longbow, and a quiver of arrows. His clothing, made from various animal skins and grasses, was sophisticated, featuring a bearskin cap, deerskin quiver, and shoes insulated with grass.

Forensic analyses have pieced together the final moments of his life. Ötzi died from an arrow wound to his left shoulder, likely the result of a violent confrontation. Additionally, his body bore numerous tattoos, which some researchers believe may have been part of a primitive form of acupuncture used to relieve pain from chronic ailments like arthritis.

The story of Ötzi took a darker turn as those who were involved in the discovery and study of his remains began to experience untimely and mysterious deaths. This series of unfortunate events led to the belief in a so-called *Curse of Ötzi*.

1. Rainer Henn - The forensic pathologist who placed Ötzi in a body bag died in a car accident en route to a conference about the Iceman.
2. Kurt Fritz - The mountaineer who guided Henn to Ötzi's body died in an avalanche.
3. Helmut Simon - One of Ötzi's discoverers, died from a fall during a hike.
4. Dieter Warnecke - The head of the rescue team that searched for Simon, died of a heart attack shortly after Simon's funeral.
5. Konrad Spindler - The leading Ötzi expert,

who dismissed the curse as media hype,
succumbed to multiple sclerosis.

In total, seven deaths have been linked to the curse,
each involving individuals who had close contact with
Ötzi. While some see these events as evidence of a
supernatural curse, others argue that the deaths are coincidental, highlighting the risks associated with alpine
exploration and the natural vulnerabilities of those
involved.

Today, Ötzi's remains are housed at the South Tyrol
Museum of Archaeology in Bolzano, Italy, where they are
kept in a specially designed cold chamber to mimic the
glacial environment in which he was found. Visitors can
view Ötzi through a small window, along with various artifacts that provide further context about his life and era.

Ötzi has permeated popular culture, inspiring documentaries, museum exhibits, and even fictional works.
His story has sparked the imagination of many, leading to
dramatizations and speculative fiction about his life and
the supposed curse.

From a scientific perspective, the notion of a curse is
often viewed with skepticism. The deaths linked to Ötzi
can largely be attributed to natural causes and the
inherent dangers of working in harsh environments. For
instance, the avalanche that claimed Kurt Fritz's life is a
known hazard for mountaineers, and heart attacks and

chronic illnesses like multiple sclerosis are, unfortunately, common ailments.

Additionally, the scientific community tends to focus on the tangible contributions of Ötzi to our understanding of prehistoric life rather than the myths surrounding his discovery. The detailed forensic work, genetic studies, and continual technological advancements in studying ancient remains offer a rational counterpoint to the idea of a curse.

Ötzi the Iceman remains one of the most fascinating archaeological finds of the modern era. His well-preserved body and the artifacts found with him provide a unique window into the Copper Age, shedding light on the life, health, and technology of prehistoric humans. While tales of curses and supernatural phenomena add an element of mystery and intrigue, the true legacy of Ötzi lies in the wealth of scientific knowledge his discovery has unlocked. As we continue to study his remains with ever-evolving technology, Ötzi will undoubtedly continue to offer new insights and inspire future generations of archaeologists and historians.

CHAPTER 9

ROBERT THE DOLL

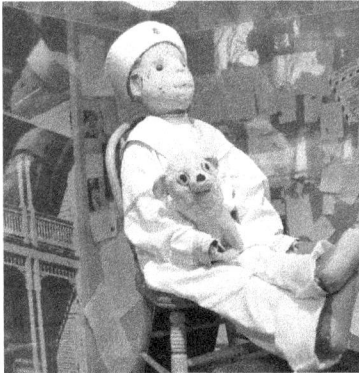

Robert the Doll at the Fort East Martello Museum in Key West, Florida.

Robert the Doll, a seemingly innocuous toy, has earned a reputation as one of the most haunted objects in the world. The story begins in the early 20th century with Robert Eugene Otto, a young boy in Key West, Florida. Eugene, who was often called "Gene," received the doll in 1904. Accounts of how Robert came into Gene's possession vary. One popular version suggests that the doll was a gift from Gene's grandfather, purchased during a trip to Germany. Another theory posits that a disgruntled servant, allegedly skilled in voodoo, gave the doll to the family as a form of retribution for some perceived wrong.

A young Robert Eugene Otto (right) wearing the sailor's suit that was eventually given to Robert the Doll.

The doll, manufactured by the Steiff Company, stands nearly 40 inches tall and is stuffed with wood wool known as excelsior. Robert's sailor suit is believed to be a hand-me-down from Gene himself, further cementing the unusual bond between boy and toy. Gene named the doll "Robert" after himself and quickly became inseparable from his new companion.

As Gene grew older, the relationship between him

and Robert became increasingly strange. Gene's parents often heard him talking to the doll, and unsettlingly, they claimed to hear a deep voice responding. This eerie inter-action was only the beginning. Soon, peculiar and disturbing events started occurring in the Otto house-hold. Furniture was found overturned, and toys muti-lated, with Gene consistently blaming Robert for the chaos. These claims were initially dismissed as childhood imagination, but the incidents escalated, causing alarm among family members and visitors alike.

One particularly chilling account involves a plumber who was working in the Otto home. He reported hearing children's laughter, despite being alone in the house. Upon investigating, he noticed that Robert had moved from one side of the room to the other, and objects that were previously in the doll's lap had mysteriously been thrown across the room.

Gene's attachment to Robert persisted into adult-hood. After studying art in major cities like Chicago, New York, and Paris, Gene returned to Key West with his wife, Anne. They moved into his childhood home, which Gene named "The Artist House." Despite his wife's discomfort with the doll, Gene insisted on keeping Robert, designating a special room for him in the attic. Anne reportedly felt uneasy around Robert and requested that he be locked away. Nevertheless, Robert frequently appeared in the window of an upstairs room, seemingly defying efforts to confine him to the attic.

Locals began avoiding the house, claiming to see Robert move from one window to another and hearing unexplained footsteps and laughter emanating from within. The legend of the haunted doll spread, with many attributing misfortunes to interactions with Robert.

After Gene's death in 1974, the house was sold to Myrtle Reuter, who also experienced strange occurrences with Robert. She lived with the doll for 20 years, during which she reported hearing footsteps and laughter, and noticing changes in the doll's facial expressions. Finally, in 1994, she donated Robert to the Fort East Martello Museum in Key West, where he resides to this day.

The museum staff initially dismissed Reuter's claims, but soon they too experienced unusual phenomena. Cameras and electronic devices malfunctioned in Robert's presence, and visitors reported feeling uneasy. The museum began receiving letters addressed to Robert, often apologies from those who believed they had disrespected him during their visit and subsequently suffered misfortunes.

While the legend of Robert the Doll is rich in supernatural lore, there are plausible scientific explanations for some of the reported phenomena. The power of suggestion and the psychological effects of expectation can lead people to perceive ordinary occurrences as supernatural. For instance, the movement of the doll could be attributed to vibrations from passing traffic or changes in temperature causing slight shifts in position.

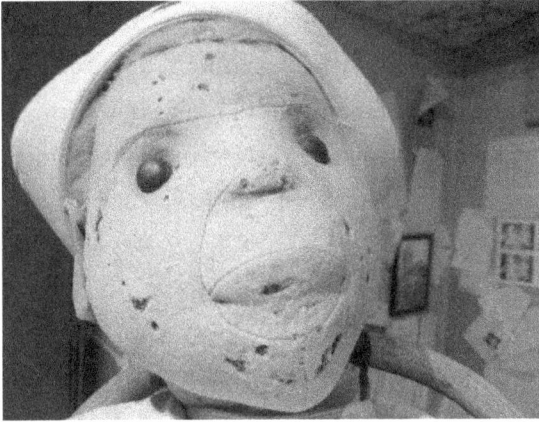

Moreover, the human brain is adept at recognizing patterns and faces, which might explain why some people believe they see Robert's facial expressions change. The doll's infamous reputation also plays a significant role, as visitors might be primed to experience something eerie, amplifying otherwise mundane events into something sinister.

Robert the Doll has left an indelible mark on popular culture. He has inspired films, such as the "Robert" series, which began in 2015, and has been featured in numerous television shows and documentaries, including "Ghost Adventures: Artifacts." His story has been the subject of podcasts and books, further cementing his status as a cultural icon of the paranormal.

The legend of Robert the Doll is a compelling mix of historical facts, folklore, and psychological phenomena. While the accounts of supernatural activity are intriguing, they can often be explained by natural causes and the power of suggestion. Whether one believes in the hauntings or views them as products of imagination, Robert's tale continues to captivate and terrify audiences around the world. The enduring fascination with Robert the Doll speaks to our deep-seated curiosity and fear of the unknown.

While I remain skeptical of the supernatural claims, the story of Robert the Doll is a fascinating example of how folklore and human psychology can intertwine to create enduring legends.

CHAPTER 10

THE WINCHESTER MYSTERY HOUSE

The Winchester Mystery House, located in San Jose, California, is an architectural marvel and one of the most famous haunted houses in America. Its origins trace back to Sarah Winchester, the widow of William Wirt

Winchester, heir to the Winchester Repeating Arms Company.

Sarah inherited a substantial fortune after her husband's death in 1881, including a 50% ownership in the company and an income of $1,000 a day (equivalent to approximately $27,000 today).

In 1886, Sarah Winchester purchased an eight-room farmhouse and began an ambitious

William Wirt Winchester

Sarah Winchester, 1865

and continuous building project that lasted 38 years until her death in 1922. The construction of the house was driven by a combination of grief, guilt, and possibly spiritual beliefs. According to legend, Sarah Winchester was haunted by the spirits of those killed by Winchester rifles. A medium purportedly told her that to appease these spirits and avoid their vengeance, she must build a house for them and never stop the construction.

The Winchester Mystery House is renowned for its bizarre and intricate design. The mansion originally spanned seven stories, though an earthquake in 1906 reduced it to its current four stories. The house contains 160 rooms, 47 fireplaces, 10,000 panes of glass, two basements, and three elevators.

Stairs to nowhere

The architectural oddities of the house include staircases that lead to nowhere, doors that open into walls, windows that overlook other rooms, and a skylight in the floor. Sarah Winchester's designs were highly unconventional and lacked a master plan, leading to a labyrinthine structure meant to confuse spirits.

One of the most famous features is the "Door to Nowhere," a door that opens outward to a sheer drop from an upper floor. The house also boasts luxurious amenities rare for its time, including indoor plumbing, hot running water, and push-button gas lighting.

The Winchester Mystery House is steeped in legends of hauntings and supernatural occurrences. Sarah Winchester herself is believed to haunt the mansion, with many visitors and employees reporting sightings of her apparition. Her ghost is often seen in her bedroom or gazing out of windows.

The 'Door to Nowhere'

Other reported hauntings include the "Wheelbarrow Ghost," a spectral handyman seen pushing a wheelbarrow in the basement or performing repairs. Visitors and staff have also reported hearing disembodied voices, footsteps, and seeing shadowy figures throughout the mansion.

The types of hauntings reported at the Winchester Mystery House include residual hauntings, where events from the past seem to replay like a loop, and intelligent hauntings, where spirits interact with the living. Shadow figures are the most commonly reported phenomenon, appearing in hallways and windows.

Numerous paranormal investigators have explored the Winchester Mystery House, capturing electronic voice phenomena (EVPs), experiencing sudden temperature drops, and witnessing unexplained movements of objects. Long-time maintenance worker Denny reported hearing footsteps that seemed to follow him around the mansion but always stayed one step ahead.

Personal accounts from visitors include feelings of being touched by invisible hands, hearing whispers in empty rooms, and seeing doorknobs turn on their own. These experiences contribute to the house's lore and its reputation as one of America's most haunted places.

While many believe in the hauntings of the Winchester Mystery House, others view the stories as a product of imagination fueled by the house's eerie atmosphere and Sarah Winchester's enigmatic life. Skeptics argue that the mansion's strange design and Sarah's reclusiveness led to the creation of ghost stories to attract tourists and add mystique to the property.

Some historians suggest that Sarah Winchester's continuous construction was more about philanthropy and keeping herself occupied rather than an attempt to appease spirits. She employed many workers and artisans, contributing to the local economy, and her architectural endeavors might have been a means to cope with her grief.

Movie poster for, Winchester.
Courtesy of Lionsgate

Today, the Winchester Mystery House is a popular tourist attraction, drawing visitors with its haunted reputation and architectural curiosity. It has been featured in numerous television shows, documentaries, and movies. The 2018 film, *Winchester*, starring Helen Mirren, dramatizes Sarah Winchester's life and the construction of the house, further cementing its place in popular culture.

The house continues to offer guided tours, including special flashlight tours that enhance the spooky experience. It remains a symbol of the intersection between history, mystery, and the supernatural, captivating all who visit its labyrinthine halls.

Whether one views it as a haunted mansion, an architectural oddity, or a historical curiosity, it undeniably captures the imagination. The house's legacy invites reflection on the unseen forces that shape our lives and the lengths to which we might go to make peace with them.

CHAPTER 11

THE BLACK ORLOV DIAMOND

The Black Orlov Diamond, also known as the Eye of Brahma, is a rare black diamond weighing 67.50 carats. Its origins are steeped in legend and mystery. The story begins in 19th-century India, where the diamond was allegedly one of the eyes adorning a statue of the Hindu god Brahma in a shrine near Pondicherry. According to lore, a monk stole the 195-carat uncut diamond from the statue, an act considered a grave sacrilege. This theft is said to have triggered the curse associated with the diamond, causing misfortune to all who possessed it.

The Black Orlov resurfaced in the early 20th century when it was purchased by J.W. Paris, a diamond dealer, in 1932. Paris brought the diamond to the United States, but shortly after securing its sale, he reportedly committed suicide by jumping from a New York skyscraper. This tragic event is often cited as the first instance of the diamond's curse taking effect.

Subsequent owners included two Russian princesses, Leonila Galitsine-Bariatinsky and Nadia Vyegin-Orlov, who both allegedly committed suicide by jumping to their deaths in the 1940s. However, historical records and the identities of these princesses are dubious, leading some to question the veracity of these stories.

Black diamonds, or carbonado diamonds, are rare and have unique physical properties compared to traditional clear diamonds. They are primarily found in Brazil and Central Africa, not India, which casts doubt on the supposed origin of the Black Orlov. These diamonds contain inclusions of other minerals and exhibit a poly-crystalline structure, which contributes to their distinctive dark color.

Eyewitness accounts of the Black Orlov's curse are largely anecdotal. While the suicides of J.W. Paris and the Russian princesses add to the diamond's mystique, concrete evidence linking these events to the diamond is lacking. The stories of the princesses, in particular, are difficult to verify, as the records do not corroborate their existence or their connection to the diamond.

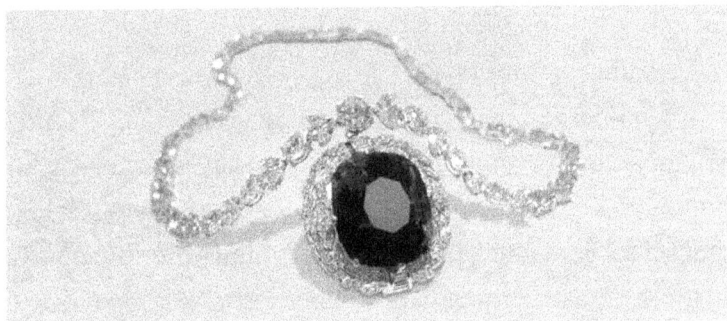

The Black Orlov was later acquired by Charles F. Wilson, who had it recut into three pieces in an attempt to break the curse. The largest piece, weighing 67.50 carats, was set into a brooch surrounded by 108 diamonds and suspended from a necklace containing 124 diamonds. The diamond has since been displayed in various museums, including the American Museum of Natural History in New York and the Natural History Museum in London.

In 2006, the Black Orlov was featured in a Christie's auction, though its current owner remains undisclosed. The diamond's last known public appearance was in the form of a platinum and diamond necklace, highlighting its enduring allure despite its dark reputation.

The Black Orlov has captured public imagination and has been referenced in various media. Its dramatic history and supposed curse have made it a subject of intrigue in books, documentaries, and articles about cursed gemstones. The diamond's notoriety is comparable to other famous cursed diamonds like the Hope Diamond and the Koh-i-Noor, each with its own tales of misfortune and mystery.

While the stories surrounding the Black Orlov Diamond are fascinating, they are largely based on legend and anecdotal evidence. The supposed curse lacks scientific backing, and many details about the diamond's history remain unverifiable. The association of tragic events with the diamond could be coincidental, and the allure of a good story often perpetuates such myths. Skeptics point out that the narratives surrounding cursed diamonds often serve as publicity stunts to increase their mystique and value.

While the Black Orlov Diamond is a remarkable gemstone with a captivating story, there is no concrete evidence to support the claims of it being cursed. The tales of misfortune linked to the diamond are likely exaggerated or fabricated, making it more a piece of captivating folklore than a genuinely cursed object.

CHAPTER 12
THE BASANO VASE

The Basano Vase, often touted as one of the most cursed objects in history, is believed to have originated in the 15th century in a small town north of Naples, Italy. The vase is made of silver, a material traditionally associated with purity and protection, which makes its cursed reputation all the more paradoxical. The legend surrounding the Basano Vase begins with a young bride who received it as a wedding gift. Tragically, she died on her wedding night under mysterious circumstances, reportedly holding the vase in her hands as she drew her last breath. According to the tale, with her dying breath, she vowed vengeance, and it is this promise that is said to have imbued the vase with its malevolent power.

Following the bride's death, the vase was passed down through her family. Each successive owner reportedly met an untimely end, dying soon after taking possession of the vase. This pattern of death continued until the family, desperate to end the cycle of tragedy, hid the vase away. The exact location where the vase was hidden remained a mystery, shrouded in layers of folklore and speculation.

The vase re-emerged in 1988 when it was discovered by an unnamed man who unearthed it from an undisclosed location. Inside the vase, he found a note warning:

Beware... This vase brings death.

Ignoring the ominous message, the man brought the vase to an auction house where it quickly sold for a significant sum. The buyer, a local pharmacist, died under mysterious circumstances three months later. The vase was then sold to a surgeon who similarly died shortly after acquiring it. The cycle of death continued with each new owner, including an archaeologist and a few other buyers, all of whom died within a few months of taking possession of the vase.

Eyewitness accounts of the vase's cursed effects are varied and often inconsistent. Some reports suggest that the vase was responsible for a series of sudden, unexplained deaths, while others claim that those who came into contact with the vase experienced a sense of impending doom and severe misfortune.

Scientific explanations for the alleged curse have been speculative at best. Some skeptics suggest that the deaths associated with the vase could be coincidental or could be attributed to natural causes. Another theory posits that the vase, if buried for centuries, might have harbored harmful substances like mold or bacteria that could cause severe health issues. However, no concrete evidence has been presented to substantiate these claims.

One intriguing aspect of the Basano Vase story is the material from which it is made. Silver, historically considered a metal with protective qualities against evil, seems an unlikely medium for a cursed object. This contradiction has led some to question the authenticity of the curse and suggest that the legend may have been embellished or fabricated entirely.

The current whereabouts of the Basano Vase are unknown. After the last known owner died, the vase was reportedly thrown out of a window by a family member, hitting a passing police officer. Attempts to donate the vase to museums were unsuccessful, as no institution wanted to risk housing a cursed object. The officer eventually buried the vase in a lead box in a secret location, likely on consecrated ground, to prevent further tragedies.

Despite its chilling legend, the Basano Vase has not garnered as much attention in popular culture as other cursed objects like the Hope Diamond or the Dybbuk Box. It does, however, frequently appear on lists of the world's most haunted or cursed items and has been featured in various articles and books exploring paranormal phenomena and haunted artifacts.

The story of the Basano Vase is compelling, filled with elements of mystery, tragedy, and the supernatural. However, a critical examination of the tale reveals several inconsistencies and gaps in the narrative. The absence of verifiable details, such as the names of the individuals involved and specific locations, casts doubt on the authenticity of the curse. Furthermore, the vase's supposed reappearance in 1988, complete with a dramatic warning note, seems almost too convenient and could suggest a fabrication aimed at increasing the object's value at auction.

The legend's reliance on a series of unexplained deaths also raises questions. While it is true that several individuals associated with the vase reportedly died under mysterious circumstances, the lack of medical records or autopsy reports makes it difficult to ascertain the true causes of these deaths. Additionally, the notion that no museum would accept the vase due to its cursed reputation is questionable, given that many institutions house artifacts with similar legends.

While the Basano Vase's story is fascinating and eerie, it is likely that the tale has been exaggerated over time. The vase may indeed have a dark history, but the lack of concrete evidence and the many inconsistencies in the narrative suggest that the legend of the Basano Vase is more myth than reality. Whether or not the vase is truly cursed, its tale continues to captivate and intrigue those who hear it, ensuring that its legacy endures.

Paula Jean Welden

The disappearance of Paula Jean Welden on December 1, 1946, is one of the most enduring mysteries in Vermont's history. An 18-year-old sophomore at Bennington College, Paula vanished while hiking on the Long Trail, a 273-mile

hiking route that extends through the forests and mountains of Vermont. Despite extensive searches and numerous
theories, no trace of her has ever been found. Her case not
only captivated the nation but also led to significant
changes in the state's law enforcement infrastructure.

Paula Jean Welden was a typical college student in many
respects. She was studying art at Bennington College,
though she had expressed interest in switching her major
to botany. She worked part-time in the college dining hall
and was known to be an adventurous and outdoorsy
young woman who enjoyed hiking, camping, and other
outdoor activities.

On the afternoon of December 1, 1946, Paula told her

roommate that she was going to take a break from studying and go for a hike on the Long Trail. She left Dewey Hall at approximately 2:30 PM, wearing a red parka, blue jeans, and white sneakers—not the most suitable attire for the cold weather. Paula had little money with her, having left behind an uncashed check from her parents.

Paula was last seen hitchhiking near the Bennington campus around 2:45 PM, where a motorist gave her a ride to the trailhead near Glastenbury Mountain. Several witnesses saw her walking along the trail later that afternoon. One of the last people to see her was a man named Louis Knapp, who spoke with her around 4:00 PM. She asked him about the trail's length before continuing on her way.

The sun set around 5:00 PM, and shortly afterward, it began to snow. Paula did not return to her dormitory that evening, but her roommate assumed she was studying late. It was only the next morning, when she failed to attend her classes, that Paula was reported missing.

The search for Paula was immediate but disorganized, largely due to Vermont's lack of a state police force at the time. The college organized search parties composed of students and faculty, but their efforts were hampered by the snowy conditions and lack of proper equipment. As days passed with no sign of Paula, the search expanded to include firefighters, the National Guard, and even the Connecticut State Police.

Paula's father, Archibald Welden, was particularly critical of the local authorities' handling of the search. He enlisted the help of Governor Ernest Gibson, who called in additional support from neighboring states. Despite these efforts, no trace of Paula was ever found on or near the trail.

In the days following Paula's disappearance, several eyewitnesses came forward with potential leads. A waitress in Fall River, Massachusetts, claimed to have seen a disturbed young woman matching Paula's description in a diner the day after she vanished, but this lead proved inconclusive. A train conductor reported seeing her in South Carolina, but this too led nowhere.

One of the more intriguing leads involved a man named Fred Gadette, a lumberjack who lived near the Long Trail. Gadette reportedly made several conflicting statements about his whereabouts on the day Paula disappeared and even claimed to know where she was buried. However, he later recanted these statements, claiming he was seeking attention. Despite being considered a person of interest, no evidence was found to link him to Paula's disappearance.

Over the years, numerous theories have emerged regarding Paula's fate. These range from the plausible to the fantastical:

1. Accidental Death: One of the most straightforward theories is that Paula got lost or injured on the trail and succumbed to the elements. The sudden snowfall and cold temperatures would have made survival difficult without proper gear.

2. Suicide: Some have speculated that Paula may have been depressed and chose to end her life in the wilderness. However, those who knew her, including her family, refuted this theory, citing her generally positive outlook and future plans.

3. Foul Play: Given the lack of evidence, many believe Paula met with foul play. Suspects include local residents like Fred Gadette and others who might have encountered her on the trail. However, without any physical evidence, this theory remains speculative.

4. Voluntary Disappearance: Another theory is that Paula chose to disappear and start a new life elsewhere. Supporters of this theory point to the fact that she had been feeling stressed about her studies and future. Yet, those close to her found this highly unlikely.

5. The Bennington Triangle: Paula's disappearance is one of several mysterious vanishings in the Bennington area between 1945 and 1950. This cluster of disappearances has led some to speculate about supernatural or paranormal causes, dubbing the area the "Bennington Triangle".

The mishandling of Paula Jean Welden's case had significant repercussions. Her father and others pushed for the establishment of a professional state law enforcement agency, leading to the creation of the Vermont State Police in 1947. This was one positive outcome from an otherwise tragic situation.

Paula's disappearance has remained a topic of interest and speculation for decades. It inspired several works of fiction, including Shirley Jackson's novel "Hangsaman" and Hillary Waugh's "Last Seen Wearing...".

❦

The case of Paula Jean Welden is a haunting reminder of how easily a person can vanish without a trace. Despite extensive searches, numerous theories, and ongoing interest, Paula's fate remains a mystery. Her disappearance not only impacted her family and community but also led to significant changes in Vermont's approach to law enforcement and search and rescue operations. As the years go by, the hope for answers persists, keeping Paula Jean Welden's story alive in the annals of unsolved mysteries.

❦

VANISHED: STRANGE & MYSTERIOUS DISAPPEARANCES

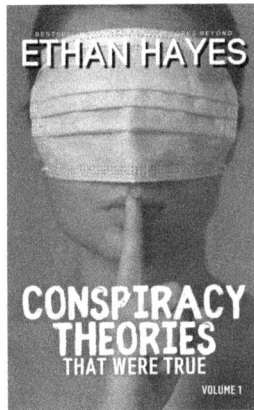

TUSKEGEE SYPHILIS EXPERIMENT

The Tuskegee Syphilis Experiment, also known as the Tuskegee Study of Untreated Syphilis in the Negro Male, is one of the most infamous cases of unethical human experimentation in U.S. history, and at one time was considered a conspiracy theory. The study was initially supposed to last six months but ended up continuing for 40 years, from 1932 to 1972.

⚜

ORIGINS:

The study began in 1932 in Macon County, Alabama, and was conducted by the U.S. Public Health Service (USPHS).

Dr. Taliaferro Clark was the original architect of the study. Initially, Dr. Clark intended the study to be a short-term project to record the progression of syphilis and then offer treatment. However, under subsequent leadership, the study's purpose shifted to observing the long-term effects of untreated syphilis.

KEY FIGURES / INSTITUTIONS OVER THE YEARS:

The initiation and continuation of the Tuskegee Syphilis Experiment were facilitated by a combination of institutional decisions by the USPHS, complicit actions by key individuals, and the broader societal context of racial discrimination and unequal access to healthcare. The study's prolonged duration, despite clear ethical violations, is a testament to the systemic issues that allowed such an experiment to persist for four decades.

- **Dr. Raymond Vonderlehr**: He succeeded Dr. Clark and became the on-site director of the study. Under his leadership, the intention of the study was redefined to observe untreated syphilis in black males until their deaths. Vonderlehr developed the procedures for the study and was involved in its operations for many years.
- **Dr. John Heller**: He was another central figure in the study who directed it for a significant portion of its duration, particularly during the years after World War II. Under his tenure, the withholding of treatment continued, even after penicillin was recognized as a standard and effective treatment for syphilis.
- **Dr. Oliver Wenger**: While not directly overseeing the study, Wenger was a key figure in the USPHS's venereal disease section and supported the Tuskegee experiment.
- **Tuskegee Institute**: The Tuskegee Institute (now Tuskegee University), a historically black college in Alabama, played a role in the study. The USPHS collaborated with the Institute, which provided logistical support and helped gain the trust of the local community. However, it's essential to note that the primary responsibility and decision-making

authority for the study's design and continuation lay with the USPHS.

- **Dr. Eugene Dibble**: He was the head of the John Andrew Hospital at the Tuskegee Institute and was involved in the study, mainly in its early stages.
- **Eunice Rivers**: She was a black nurse who played a significant role in the day-to-day operations of the study. Rivers was responsible for maintaining contact with the participants, ensuring they attended scheduled appointments, and acted as a bridge between the researchers and the community. Because of her involvement and trust within the community, many participants stayed in the study.

MAIN FEATURES OF THE EXPERIMENT:

The study involved 600 black men, of which 399 had syphilis and 201 did not. The men were told they were being treated for "bad blood," a colloquial term used in the community to describe several ailments, including syphilis, anemia, and fatigue.

The participants were not informed of their syphilis diagnosis nor were they informed about the study's true purpose. Instead, they were told they were receiving free healthcare, meals, and burial insurance in exchange for participating.

Even when penicillin became the standard treatment for syphilis in 1947, the men in the study were neither informed about this development nor provided with the antibiotic. Researchers intentionally withheld treatment to observe the disease's progression.

DECEPTION:

There's no documented evidence that the men in the Tuskegee Syphilis Experiment were collectively aware that they were being deceived and subsequently made public claims about the study during its early years or even much of its duration. It's essential to understand the context and the level of manipulation involved:

The participants were deceived from the start. They were told that they were being treated for "bad blood," a local term that could refer to several conditions, including syphilis, anemia, and fatigue. The U.S. Public Health Service provided them with placebos, ineffective methods, and diagnostic procedures under the guise of "treatment." Because of this, many of the men believed they were receiving genuine healthcare.

Medical authorities, especially during the time when the study began, were highly respected. The men had little reason to doubt the intentions of the health professionals involved, especially when they were provided with certain benefits like free medical check-ups and meals during examinations.

Nurse Rivers played a pivotal role in maintaining the

trust of the participants. As a Black nurse who was part of their community, she was instrumental in keeping the men involved in the study. Her relationship with the participants further ensured that they felt they were in good hands.

Many of the participants were not well-informed about syphilis, its treatments, or the broader implications of medical research. This lack of information, combined with the intentional deception by the study's conductors, made it less likely for the men to question the proceedings.

The racial dynamics of the American South in the early to mid-20th century meant that Black individuals often faced systemic racism, were marginalized, and lacked resources. Such a context might have made it even more challenging for the participants to voice concerns or seek second opinions.

EXPOSED:

The Tuskegee Syphilis Experiment became public knowledge in 1972. The unethical practices of the study were brought to national attention by Peter Buxtun, a former Public Health Service interviewer and whistle-blower. Buxtun had expressed his concerns about the study to his superiors within the USPHS several times since the late 1960s, but it was only after no internal action was taken that he decided to go to the press.

Jean Heller, a reporter for the Associated Press, broke

the story on July 25, 1972, revealing the details of the study to the general public. The article described how for four decades, the U.S. Public Health Service had deliberately withheld treatment from hundreds of black men with syphilis as part of a research experiment.

When the Tuskegee Syphilis Experiment was exposed by Jean Heller in 1972, the government did not deny the study's existence or its details. The facts were well-documented, and Peter Buxtun, the whistleblower, provided evidence about the experiment. Additionally, the U.S. Public Health Service, which had overseen the study, did not dispute the revelations once they were made public and shut it down.

However, in the immediate aftermath of the story breaking, some officials and representatives of the U.S. Public Health Service tried to justify or defend the study's intent and procedures, citing the research's importance or arguing that standards and norms had changed since the study began in 1932. This stance was not a denial but rather an attempt to provide context or justification, which was widely seen as insufficient and unsatisfactory given the gross ethical violations.

The media, for its part, generally reported on the story with shock and outrage. The revelations led to extensive media coverage, which played a crucial role in informing the public about the study's details and the ethical issues at stake.

The overwhelming negative reaction from the public,

medical community, and media alike led to congressional hearings, which culminated in a stronger framework for the protection of human subjects in research studies and ultimately the creation of institutional review boards (IRBs) to oversee and approve research involving human participants.

CONSEQUENCES AND OUTCOMES:

Many participants of the study suffered severe health complications due to untreated syphilis, and some even died from the disease. Their families also suffered, with spouses becoming infected and children born with congenital syphilis.

In 1973, a $10 million out-of-court settlement was reached, and the U.S. government promised to give life-time medical benefits and burial services to all living participants. The widows of the participants were also provided with health benefits.

In 1997, President Bill Clinton formally apologized on behalf of the U.S. government to the surviving partici-pants of the study and their families.

The experiment sowed deep distrust among many in the Black community towards the U.S. healthcare system, which still reverberates today.

ஒஜ்தூ

CONSPIRACY THEORIES THAT WERE TRUE

CHAPTER 13

CHÂTEAU DE BRISSAC

The Château de Brissac, towering majestically in the Loire Valley, is renowned not only for its grandeur but also for its ghostly resident. Originally constructed in the 11th century by the Counts of Anjou, the castle has undergone several transformations throughout its long history. After the English were defeated by King Philip

II of France, the property was given to Guillaume des Roches, marking the beginning of its storied past. In the 15th century, the château was rebuilt by Pierre de Brézé, a chief minister to King Charles VII, making it a symbol of wealth and power in the region.

Charlotte de Brézé, now known as the Green Lady

The most famous ghost story associated with the château involves Charlotte de Brézé, the illegitimate daughter of King Charles VII and his mistress, Agnes Sorel. In 1462, Charlotte married Jacques de Brézé, the lord of Château de Brissac. Despite their union producing five children, their marriage was far from happy. Charlotte, accustomed to the sophistication of court life, found the rural castle and her husband's boorish ways unbearable. She eventually sought solace in an affair with Pierre de Lavergne, one of Jacques' huntsmen.

On a fateful night in 1477, Jacques discovered the lovers together in Charlotte's chambers. In a fit of rage, he killed them both, purportedly inflicting multiple wounds with his sword. The gruesome nature of their deaths has fueled the castle's haunted reputation. It is said that Jacques moved out of the castle soon after, unable to bear the haunting wails and apparitions of his murdered wife.

Charlotte de Brézé's chambers

Charlotte de Brézé, now known as the "Green Lady" due to the green dress she is often seen wearing, is said to haunt the tower room of the château's chapel. Visitors and residents alike have reported sightings of her spectral form, described as having holes where her eyes and nose should be, reflecting the brutal injuries she suffered. Her ghostly presence is often accompanied by mournful moans in the early hours, perpetuating the eerie atmosphere of the château.

While the tales of the Green Lady are compelling, scientific explanations for such phenomena often point to environmental factors. Some researchers suggest that infrasound, which are low-frequency sound waves, can cause feelings of unease, anxiety, and even visual hallucinations. Old buildings like Château de Brissac, with their creaking floors and whistling winds, might create such sounds, contributing to the haunting experiences reported.

Moreover, the power of suggestion plays a significant role in perceived hauntings. When visitors are aware of the château's ghostly reputation, their minds are primed to interpret any unusual occurrences—such as drafts, creaks, or distant noises—as supernatural events.

Many visitors have shared their spine-chilling encounters at Château de Brissac. One common story involves guests waking up to the sight of a woman in a green dress standing at the foot of their bed, her face a horrifying spectacle. Others have heard inexplicable wailing and felt sudden drops in temperature, particularly in the tower room of the chapel where Charlotte was murdered.

The current owners, the Cossé-Brissac family, have also acknowledged the ghostly presence. They have grown accustomed to Charlotte's ghost, which they claim to have seen on numerous occasions. Despite these eerie experiences, they continue to live in and maintain the château, welcoming curious tourists and paranormal enthusiasts alike.

Today, Château de Brissac stands as the tallest château in France, with seven floors and 204 rooms. It is managed by Charles-André de Cossé-Brissac, the 14th Duke of Brissac. The château is open to the public for tours, allowing visitors to explore its lavish interiors, historic art collections, and the legendary haunted chapel.

The château's gardens are a serene contrast to its haunted reputation. Featuring over 450 types of roses, mazes, fountains, and sculptures, they provide a peaceful retreat for visitors. The extensive wine cellars offer a taste of the Loire Valley's finest wines, adding to the château's allure.

Château de Brissac has made its mark in popular culture as well. It was featured in the mid-1990s as a venue for the French Battles of the original Japanese Iron Chef television show. More recently, the château has appeared in various documentaries and ghost-hunting shows, drawing international attention to its haunted history.

With its rich history and the legend of the Green Lady, the Château de Brissac remains one of France's most intriguing and mysterious landmarks. Whether one believes in ghosts or not, the château offers a fascinating glimpse into the past and a hauntingly beautiful experience for all who visit.

CHAPTER 14
THE CONJURED CHEST

The tale of the Conjured Chest begins in the 1830s in Meade County, Kentucky. The chest, an Empire-style mahogany dresser, was commissioned by Jeremiah Graham, a wealthy plantation owner. Graham tasked his enslaved craftsman, Remus, with creating the chest for the arrival of his firstborn child. However, upon its completion, Graham was dissatisfied with the piece and, in a fit of rage, beat Remus to death. Seeking retribution for Remus's unjust death, the other slaves on the plantation allegedly performed a ritual involving owl blood, cursing the chest to bring death or great misfortune to anyone who used it.

The first tragedy struck soon after when Graham's newborn died in infancy. Over the following decades, the chest was passed down through the Graham family, leaving a trail of sorrow and death. By the time Virginia Hudson Cleveland inherited it from her grandmother Eliza Gregory, the chest was blamed for at least 16 deaths and several other tragedies, including serious injuries and illnesses. Determined to break the curse, Cleveland and her maid, Sallie, performed a counter-ritual using a dead owl. Sallie died shortly afterward, but it remains unclear if the curse was truly lifted, as no one dared to place clothes in the chest again.

The history of the Conjured Chest is filled with eyewitness accounts and testimonies from those who encountered its deadly influence. Members of the Graham family recounted numerous tragedies attributed to the chest. One neighbor, who briefly used the chest, reportedly died soon after. These incidents cemented the chest's reputation as a cursed object within the community.

Virginia Cary Hudson Mayne, Cleveland's daughter,

inherited the chest and eventually donated it to the Kentucky Historical Society in 1976 to prevent further harm. Her daughter, Beverly Mayne Kienzle, later appeared on Zak Bagans' show "Deadly Possessions," recounting the chest's dark history and the reason behind its donation. This public disclosure helped to solidify the chest's infamous status in modern pop culture.

From a scientific standpoint, the claims of curses and hauntings can often be attributed to psychological and environmental factors rather than supernatural ones. The phenomenon known as the "curse of the pharaohs" and similar legends often involve a combination of coincidence, the power of suggestion, and the human tendency to link unrelated events to a common cause. In the case of the Conjured Chest, the tragic deaths and misfortunes could potentially be explained by natural causes or misattributions of blame in a time when medical science was not as advanced.

Skeptics argue that the belief in the chest's curse could create a self-fulfilling prophecy. Fear and expectation of misfortune can lead individuals to interpret ordinary misfortunes as being caused by the curse, reinforcing the belief in its power. Additionally, the placebo effect might cause people to experience real physical symptoms if they believe strongly enough in the curse's power.

Today, the Conjured Chest resides safely in the

Kentucky Historical Society's museum, where it is preserved as an artifact of local legend and historical interest. The chest is not only a piece of antique furniture but also a cultural relic that offers insight into the beliefs and fears of past generations. It serves as a reminder of the power of folklore and the ways in which stories can shape our understanding of the world.

Visitors to the museum can view the chest and learn about its storied past through exhibits and educational materials. The museum staff handles the chest with care, respecting both its historical significance and the fearsome reputation that precedes it.

The Conjured Chest has made appearances in various media, most notably in paranormal reality TV shows. Its feature on "Deadly Possessions" brought its eerie history to a wider audience, adding to its mystique and drawing the interest of those fascinated by haunted objects and curses. These appearances have contributed to the chest's status as a notable piece of haunted history in American folklore.

While the stories surrounding the Conjured Chest are undeniably compelling, it is crucial to approach such tales with a critical mind. The historical context and eyewitness testimonies provide a rich narrative, but they also highlight the human propensity to connect unrelated events and create stories that explain the inexplicable.

From a rational perspective, the tragedies associated with the chest can likely be attributed to natural causes and the psychological effects of belief in a curse. The fear and expectation of misfortune could have influenced the behavior and perceptions of those who came into contact with the chest, leading to a self-perpetuating cycle of belief and confirmation bias.

The Conjured Chest remains a fascinating and eerie piece of history as well as a testament to the power of storytelling and human psychology than to any supernatural force. The legacy of the chest continues to captivate and terrify, serving as a potent reminder of the enduring power of folklore and the human need to make sense of the world through stories.

FOR FURTHER READING AND EXPLORATION OF THE Conjured Chest's history, you can visit the Kentucky Historical Society's website or watch episodes of "Deadly Possessions" featuring Beverly Mayne Kienzle's accounts.

CHAPTER 15

THE MYRTLES PLANTATION MIRROR

The Myrtles Plantation in St. Francisville, Louisiana, is renowned for its rich history and infamous hauntings, with one of the most eerie tales revolving around a mirror that supposedly holds the spirits of Sara Woodruff and her children.

The story of the Myrtles Plantation begins with its construction in 1796 by General David Bradford. The plantation has changed hands multiple times, with each owner contributing to its storied past. The most notorious period came under the ownership of Judge Clark Woodruff, whose wife Sara and children allegedly met a tragic end due to poisoning by a slave named Chloe. According to legend, Chloe poisoned a birthday cake to exact revenge or regain favor after being demoted from the house. However, historical records debunk parts of this tale, revealing no evidence of a slave named Chloe and indicating that Sara and her children likely died of yellow fever rather than poisoning.

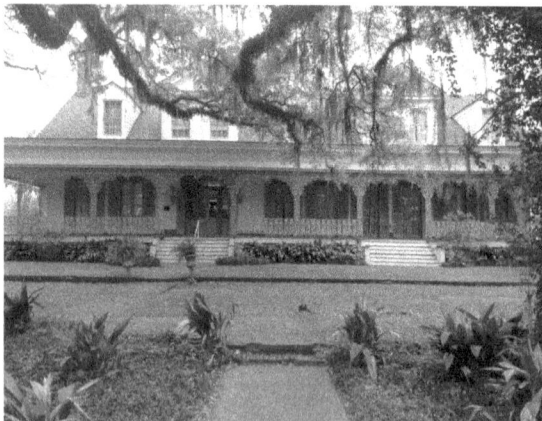

The cursed mirror is said to have entered the folklore when it was left uncovered after the deaths of Sara and her children. According to custom, mirrors are covered after a death to prevent spirits from becoming trapped. However, this particular mirror was allegedly overlooked, trapping the souls of the deceased. Visitors have reported seeing figures and handprints that cannot be wiped away, suggesting the presence of spirits.

Over the years, many guests and staff at the Myrtles Plantation have reported various paranormal experiences. The most common reports involve seeing figures in the mirror and discovering inexplicable handprints. Some visitors have also claimed to see ghostly apparitions of children in period clothing, further fueling the legend of the trapped spirits.

One of the more famous ghost sightings was captured in 1992 when the plantation owner took a photograph for insurance purposes. Upon later examination, the image allegedly showed the figure of a young girl, believed to be Chloe. This photograph became a significant piece of evidence for those who believe in the haunting.

Additional paranormal activities at the Myrtles include sightings of a young girl who died in 1868, reportedly treated by a voodoo practitioner, whose spirit is often seen in the room now known as the "Haunted Mirror Room." Guests have also reported hearing the sounds of children crying and the ghost of William Winter, who was shot on the front porch and allegedly crawled to the seventeenth step before dying.

*Alleged photo of the ghost of Chloe at Myrtles
Plantation with the figure circled.*

Despite the compelling stories and eyewitness accounts, skeptics argue that many of the tales surrounding the Myrtles Plantation can be attributed to folklore and psychological suggestions. The power of suggestion, combined with the plantation's eerie ambiance, could lead visitors to perceive ordinary reflections and smudges as ghostly apparitions. Additionally, the historical inaccuracies in the Chloe story suggest that some elements of the hauntings may be fabricated or exaggerated .

From a scientific standpoint, there is no concrete evidence to support the existence of ghosts or spirits trapped in mirrors. Many reported experiences can be explained by natural phenomena such as drafts causing reflections to shift or the human brain's tendency to recognize patterns, leading to the perception of faces or figures in random marks and smudges.

Today, the Myrtles Plantation operates as a bed and breakfast, attracting both history enthusiasts and ghost hunters. The mirror remains a focal point of the plantation's haunted tours, drawing visitors eager to glimpse the purported spirits. The plantation has been featured in numerous television shows, documentaries, and articles, further cementing its status as one of America's most haunted homes.

The Myrtles Plantation and its cursed mirror have also inspired various books and films, including appearances in paranormal investigation shows such as "Ghost Hunters" and "Unsolved Mysteries." These portrayals often emphasize the plantation's ghostly legends, contributing to its mystique and allure.

The legend of the Myrtles Plantation mirror, like many ghost stories, lies at the intersection of history, folklore, and psychological phenomena. While the eerie tales and eyewitness accounts provide a compelling narrative, the lack of verifiable evidence and historical inaccuracies suggest that much of the haunting may be the product of imagination and suggestion.

For those intrigued by the paranormal, the Myrtles Plantation offers a rich tapestry of ghostly lore to explore. Whether you believe in the hauntings or view them as stories spun from historical tragedy, the mirror at Myrtles Plantation remains an enduring symbol of the mysterious and the macabre.

CHAPTER 16
THE HANDS RESIST HIM PAINTING

"The Hands Resist Him" is a painting created by Bill Stoneham in 1972. Stoneham based the painting on a photograph taken when he was five years old, standing in front of a Chicago apartment with a neighborhood friend. The painting depicts a young boy and a female doll standing before a glass-paneled door, with numerous disembodied hands pressed against the glass from the other side. The imagery is both haunting and surreal, capturing a sense of eerie separation between the real world and a hidden realm of possibilities. Stoneham's wife wrote a poem titled "Hands Resist Him," which inspired the painting and added layers of meaning related to Stoneham's own experiences of adoption and the unknown aspects of his origin.

The painting first garnered notoriety in 2000 when it was listed on eBay by a couple who claimed it was haunted. According to the eBay listing, the figures in the painting moved at night and would even leave the canvas, scaring the couple's four-year-old daughter. They claimed to have set up a motion-activated camera which allegedly captured the boy in the painting attempting to escape. The listing included photographs purportedly showing the doll threatening the boy with what looked like a gun, but Stoneham later clarified that it was actually a battery and a tangle of wires.

The eBay auction attracted over 30,000 views and became a viral sensation. The painting eventually sold for $1,025 to Perception Gallery in Grand Rapids, Michigan. The new owners contacted Stoneham, who was surprised by the stories and strange interpretations of his work. Despite the claims of hauntings, the painting remains with Perception Gallery, which has turned down much higher offers for it.

Eyewitness accounts and anecdotal evidence further fueled the painting's reputation as haunted. Some who viewed the painting reported feeling physically ill, fainting, or experiencing unexplained phenomena. The original eBay sellers included a disclaimer warning potential buyers about the supernatural events associated with the painting. Additionally, three individuals closely linked to the painting—an art critic, a gallery owner, and an actor who initially purchased it—died under unusual circumstances within a few years of interacting with it. While these deaths can be attributed to coincidence, they have been frequently cited in discussions about the painting's purported curse.

Psychologically, the fear and discomfort associated with "The Hands Resist Him" can be explained through the concept of the "uncanny valley," where human-like figures cause unease because they are not quite lifelike. Additionally, the phenomenon of pareidolia, where people see patterns (like faces or figures) in random stimuli, might explain why viewers think the figures in the painting are moving. The human tendency to create narratives around unexplained events also plays a significant role. When an artwork like Stoneham's is associated with multiple eerie stories, our minds are primed to perceive it as haunted or cursed.

The painting remains with Perception Gallery in Grand Rapids, Michigan, and it continues to intrigue and frighten people. Bill Stoneham has painted several sequels to "The Hands Resist Him," each exploring similar themes and expanding on the original narrative. These sequels include "Resistance at the Threshold" (2004), "Threshold of Revelation" (2012), and "What Remains" (2021). Stoneham has stated that the painting and its sequels reflect his own life experiences and inner thoughts, using the recurring motifs of the glass door and disembodied hands to symbolize the barriers between different states of being and awareness.

The painting has inspired various forms of media and literature. In 2016, Darren Kyle O'Neill published a fictional book titled "The Hands Resist Him: Be Careful What You Bid For," which dramatizes the story of the painting and its eerie reputation. The painting has also been featured in numerous articles, podcasts, and documentaries exploring haunted and cursed objects. Its status as an internet legend has cemented it as a fascinating piece of modern folklore.

While the stories surrounding "The Hands Resist Him" are compelling, there is no concrete evidence to support the claims of it being haunted or cursed. The psychological explanations for why people might feel uneasy or experience strange phenomena when viewing the painting are well-grounded in scientific principles. The deaths associated with the painting can be attributed to coincidence rather than supernatural influence. Ultimately, the haunting reputation of the painting is a testament to the power of art to evoke strong emotional responses and the human propensity to create myths around unexplained events.

CHAPTER 17

JAMES DEAN'S PORSCHE 550 SPYDER
("LITTLE BASTARD")

James Dean, an iconic figure of 1950s Hollywood, was not only known for his acting prowess but also for his passion for speed. On September 21, 1955, he acquired a brand-new Porsche 550 Spyder, a sleek and powerful machine designed for racing. Dean named his car "Little Bastard," a moniker that would soon become infamous. This name was painted on the car by renowned pinstriper Dean Jeffries, adding a personal touch to the already distinctive vehicle.

Just days after purchasing the car, on September 30, 1955, Dean and his mechanic Rolf Wütherich decided to drive the Porsche to Salinas, California, to participate in a race. During the journey, they stopped at Blackwell's

Corner, where Dean met fellow racers and discussed his new vehicle. However, the trip took a tragic turn when, at approximately 5:45 PM, a young student named Donald Turnupseed made a sudden turn at an intersection on Route 466, colliding almost head-on with Dean's Porsche. Dean was pronounced dead on arrival at the Paso Robles War Memorial Hospital, while Wütherich suffered serious injuries but survived.

Following Dean's death, the wrecked Porsche was sold to George Barris, a custom car designer known for his work in Hollywood. Barris initially intended to rebuild the car but soon discovered it was beyond repair. Instead, he decided to use the car's notoriety for promotional purposes, displaying it at car shows and safety exhibitions. It was during this time that the legend of the "Little Bastard" curse began to take shape.

The first hint of the curse surfaced when the car slipped off its trailer and broke the leg of a mechanic. Subsequently, Barris sold parts of the car to various buyers, each encountering misfortune. Dr. William Eschrich, who installed the Porsche's engine in his Lotus IX, survived a serious crash. His friend, Dr. Troy McHenry, who used parts from the Porsche, was less fortunate; he lost control of his vehicle during a race and died instantly after hitting a tree.

Numerous individuals who encountered the "Little Bastard" reported eerie occurrences and feelings of unease. George Barris himself claimed that the car seemed to possess an evil presence. He recounted incidents where the car caused injuries and accidents seemingly on its own. One particularly chilling event occurred when a thief attempting to steal parts from the car slipped and broke his arm.

Several of Dean's friends, including actors Eartha Kitt and Ursula Andress, expressed their discomfort with the car, believing it to be cursed. Even before the fatal crash, these individuals refused to ride in the Porsche, citing a foreboding sense of danger.

While the stories surrounding the "Little Bastard" are compelling, they often lack scientific substantiation. Some skeptics argue that the curse is a series of coincidences amplified by the public's fascination with Dean's untimely death and the mystique of cursed objects. Psychological factors, such as the power of suggestion and confirmation bias, may also play a role in perpetuating the curse legend. When people expect bad things to happen, they are more likely to interpret events as part of the curse.

The whereabouts of the "Little Bastard" have been a mystery since 1960. After being displayed at various locations, the car was reportedly being transported to a safety exhibit when it vanished from a sealed boxcar. Despite numerous investigations and theories, the car has never been found. Some parts, such as the engine and transaxle, have resurfaced and are owned by collectors, but the main chassis remains missing.

The story of James Dean's "Little Bastard" has permeated popular culture, inspiring countless articles, documentaries, and even episodes of TV shows like "Supernatural" and "Strange World." The car's legend continues to captivate and intrigue, serving as a cautionary tale of fame, speed, and the potential consequences of tempting fate.

In 2019, Zak Bagans, a paranormal investigator and host of "Ghost Adventures," acquired the transaxle from the "Little Bastard" for his Haunted Museum in Las Vegas, further cementing the car's place in the annals of haunted history.

James Dean's Porsche 550 Spyder, "Little Bastard,"

remains one of the most infamous cursed objects in automotive history. Whether the curse is real or a product of human imagination, its impact on those who have encountered it is undeniable. The tragic fate of James Dean and the subsequent misfortunes linked to the car have created a legacy that endures, reminding us of the thin line between fascination and fear.

CHAPTER 18

THE AOKIGAHARA FOREST (SUICIDE FOREST)

Aokigahara as seen from Mount Ryu of the Tenshi Mountains

Aokigahara, also known as the Sea of Trees, is a forest at the base of Mount Fuji in Japan. This forest is not just a natural wonder; it has a deeply unsettling reputation as one of the world's most infamous locations for suicides. This chapter delves into the origins, scientific and cultural aspects, eyewitness testimonies, current status, and pop culture references of Aokigahara Forest.

⚜

AOKIGAHARA FOREST'S ORIGINS DATE BACK TO 864 CE when an eruption of Mount Fuji spewed lava across the land. Over time, this hardened lava transformed into a dense forest covering approximately 30 square kilometers. The forest is rich in biodiversity, hosting a variety of conifers and broadleaf trees, such as Japanese cypress and hemlock, which create a thick canopy that blocks out sunlight, even at noon. This contributes to the forest's eerie atmosphere, with visitors often noting the profound silence, as the porous lava bedrock absorbs sound, enhancing the sense of isolation.

Aokigahara's morbid fame as a site for suicides has historical roots intertwined with Japan's cultural views on death and suicide. Historically, suicide in Japan has often been seen through a lens of honor. Samurai would commit seppuku, a form of ritual suicide, to restore honor rather than face defeat. This cultural context has evolved, and today, suicides are more often attributed to personal struggles such as depression, financial difficulties, and social pressure.

The forest's association with death extends back centuries, with legends of ubasute, an ancient practice where elderly or infirm relatives were left in remote places to die. Although largely considered a myth, ubasute has contributed to the forest's grim reputation. The modern association with suicide began in the 1950s, and its notoriety was cemented by Seicho Matsumoto's 1960 novel *Kuroi Jukai*, which depicted lovers committing suicide in the forest. This narrative was further perpetuated by Wataru Tsurumi's 1993 book, *The Complete Manual of Suicide*, which described Aokigahara as the perfect place to die.

Visitors and local residents alike have reported unsettling experiences in Aokigahara. Many recount the oppressive silence, where even the slightest noise seems amplified. Some visitors, particularly those who stray from the established trails, have encountered abandoned personal items such as tents, shoes, and photographs, stark reminders of those who came before them intending never to leave. There are also numerous reports of discovering decomposing bodies hanging from trees or lying hidden under the forest's thick foliage.

The forest is also believed to be haunted by yūrei, or ghosts of the deceased, who are thought to wander the forest. These spirits are said to be vengeful and restless, further adding to the forest's eerie and haunted reputation. This belief in yūrei is deeply rooted in Japanese culture and mythology, contributing to the fear and respect locals have for the forest.

From a scientific standpoint, the forest's unique environment plays a role in its mystique. The dense tree cover and the lava bedrock create a natural labyrinth that is easy to get lost in. The thick vegetation and lack of wildlife contribute to the forest's silence. The moss-covered trees and the lack of sunlight create a perpetually dim and damp atmosphere, which can have psychological effects on visitors, especially those already in a fragile mental state.

In recent years, local authorities have taken measures to address the forest's dark reputation. Signs have been placed at the forest's entrance urging visitors to reconsider their actions and think of their families. These signs also provide contact information for mental health support services. Additionally, patrols by police and volunteers are conducted regularly to search for lost or suicidal individuals and to recover bodies.

Despite these efforts, Aokigahara remains a popular site for suicides, with estimates suggesting up to 100

deaths per year, though the exact numbers are no longer publicized to avoid encouraging more suicides. Security measures, such as surveillance cameras at the forest's entrance, have been implemented to monitor visitors and prevent potential suicides.

Aokigahara has captured the imagination of many and has been referenced in various forms of media. The forest was the setting for the 2015 film, *The Sea of Trees*, and the 2016 horror movie, *The Forest*, both of which explore its eerie reputation. It has also appeared in numerous books, TV shows, and even video games, often depicted as a place of mystery and supernatural occurrences.

One of the most controversial pop culture moments involving Aokigahara was the 2017 incident involving YouTuber Logan Paul, who filmed and uploaded a video of a deceased individual in the forest. The video sparked global outrage and highlighted the need for sensitivity and respect when discussing such locations.

Aokigahara Forest is a place of stark contrasts. Its natural beauty and rich biodiversity stand in sharp opposition to its reputation as a site of tragedy and despair. The forest's haunting silence, dense foliage, and cultural significance have made it a subject of fascination and fear. Efforts to mitigate its association with suicide continue, but the legends and myths surrounding Aokigahara ensure that it remains one of the most enigmatic and somber places in Japan.

Understanding Aokigahara requires a nuanced approach that considers its natural, cultural, and psychological dimensions. It serves as a powerful reminder of the importance of mental health and the need for compassion and support for those in distress.

CHAPTER 19

THE PHONE NUMBER +359 888 888 888

The phone number +359 888 888 888, issued by the Bulgarian mobile phone company Mobitel, gained infamy for allegedly being cursed. The number's first known owner was Vladimir Grashnov, the former CEO of Mobitel, who died of cancer in 2001 at the age of 48. Grashnov's death was suspiciously rapid, and some rumors suggested he had been poisoned by a business rival using radioactive materials.

Vladimir Grashnov

Following Grashnov, the number was assigned to Konstantin Dishliev, a Bulgarian real estate agent secretly involved in drug trafficking. Dishliev was shot and killed outside an Indian restaurant in 2003. The third and final owner was Konstantin Dimitrov, a Bulgarian mafia boss, who was gunned down in the Netherlands in 2005.

Scientific explanations for curses typically involve psychological and social factors rather than supernatural causes. The deaths linked to the phone number can be interpreted as coincidences or the result of the dangerous lifestyles of its owners. Grashnov's cancer could be attributed to natural causes or unrelated foul play. Dishliev and Dimitrov's deaths were likely tied to their criminal activities, making them high-risk individuals.

Konstantin Dimitrov

From a psychological perspective, belief in curses can create a self-fulfilling prophecy. If an individual believes they are cursed, their stress and anxiety can negatively impact their health and decision-making, potentially leading to dangerous situations. This phenomenon is known as the "nocebo effect," where negative expectations result in adverse outcomes.

Despite the logical explanations, the legend of the cursed phone number persists, fueled by eerie accounts and media reports. People familiar with the victims and the number recount the rapid sequence of deaths and the mysterious circumstances surrounding them. Mobitel, the issuing company, has refused to comment on the curse, stating they do not discuss individual numbers. However, they eventually suspended the number, citing unspecified reasons.

One eyewitness, a former colleague of Grashnov,

claimed that he had always been a healthy and cautious man, making his sudden illness and death particularly shocking. Friends of Dishliev and Dimitrov echoed similar sentiments, noting the abrupt and violent nature of their deaths despite their knowledge of the risks involved in their activities.

The phone number +359 888 888 888 has been permanently suspended and is no longer in use. Anyone attempting to call the number is met with a recorded message stating that it is outside network coverage. The suspension has done little to quell the rumors and superstitions, with many still believing in the curse's power.

Mobitel's decision to retire the number has only added to its mystique, leading to speculation about the company's true reasons for doing so. While the official stance is to avoid discussing individual cases, the lack of a clear explanation continues to fuel the legend.

The story of the cursed phone number has seeped into popular culture, inspiring numerous articles, blogs, and discussions on paranormal websites and forums. It is often listed among other infamous cursed objects and places, drawing parallels with legends like the Hope Diamond or the Basano Vase.

The tale has also influenced fiction, with elements of the story appearing in horror movies and novels. The concept of a cursed phone number that brings death to its owners has proven to be a compelling narrative, tapping into modern anxieties about technology and the unseen forces that may influence our lives.

The legend of +359 888 888 888 is rooted in real events, however, the scientific explanations suggest it is more likely a series of coincidences amplified by human psychology and the dangerous lifestyles of its owners. The phone number's suspension has only deepened its mystery, ensuring that the story remains a potent modern myth.

CHAPTER 20

THE TOWER OF LONDON

The Tower of London, officially known as His Majesty's Royal Palace and Fortress of the Tower of London, is a historic castle situated on the north bank of the River Thames in central London. Its origins date back to the Norman Conquest of England. William the Conqueror began construction of the White Tower in 1078, intending it to be a symbol of Norman power and dominance over the city of London. Built with limestone from

Caen in Normandy, the White Tower was both a fortress and a statement of authority.

The entire castle and fortress complex.

Throughout the centuries, the Tower of London expanded and evolved. Kings Henry III and Edward I added extensive defensive walls, towers, and a moat, transforming it into a formidable concentric castle. This fortress served not only as a royal residence but also as a treasury, armory, and prison. The Tower housed the Royal Mint until 1968 and even functioned as a menagerie for exotic animals during the medieval period.

The Tower of London is perhaps most notorious for its use as a prison, particularly for high-profile and political prisoners. Throughout its history, it has seen the imprisonment of many notable figures, including Queen

Elizabeth I before she ascended to the throne, Sir Walter Raleigh, and Guy Fawkes. The phrase "sent to the Tower" became synonymous with imprisonment and often, execution.

Torture, though not as prevalent as commonly believed, was employed within the Tower, with the infamous rack being one of the primary devices used to extract confessions. Executions, however, were more common, particularly during the turbulent times of the Tudor period. Anne Boleyn, Catherine Howard, and Lady Jane Grey are among the most famous individuals executed at the Tower.

Edward V and his brother Richard, Duke of York

The Tower of London's grim history has given rise to numerous ghost stories and legends of hauntings. One of the most enduring tales is that of the two young princes, Edward V and his brother Richard, who were imprisoned and disappeared within the Tower, presumed murdered by their uncle, Richard III. Their apparitions are said to have been seen within the Tower walls.

Another famous ghost is that of Anne Boleyn, the second wife of Henry VIII, who was executed in 1536.

Her spirit is often reported to be seen near the site of her execution and in the chapel of St. Peter ad Vincula, where she is buried.

The ghost of Lady Jane Grey, who was executed in 1554, is also said to haunt the Tower, particularly on the anniversary of her death.

Near contemporary portrait of Anne Boleyn at Hever Castle, c.1550

Eyewitness accounts of paranormal activities at the Tower of London add to its eerie reputation. Yeoman Warders, commonly known as Beefeaters, who guard the Tower, have reported strange

Lady Jane Grey

occurrences, such as unexplained footsteps, eerie lights, and sudden temperature drops. Tourists and visitors also frequently share stories of ghostly sightings and inexplicable sensations of dread.

While scientific investigations into these claims often attribute such experiences to psychological factors and the power of suggestion, the Tower's long and brutal history makes it fertile ground for ghost stories. Skeptics argue that the Tower's reputation influences perceptions, leading people to interpret normal environmental phenomena as supernatural.

Today, the Tower of London is one of the United Kingdom's most popular tourist attractions, drawing millions of visitors annually. It is maintained by Historic Royal Palaces, a charity that looks after the Tower and other historic sites. The Tower houses the Crown Jewels, a symbol of the British monarchy's continuity and grandeur, and remains a ceremonial and cultural icon.

In popular culture, the Tower of London has been featured in numerous films, television shows, and books, further cementing its status as a symbol of historical intrigue and supernatural mystery. Its stories of royalty, imprisonment, and execution have inspired works ranging from Shakespeare's plays to modern horror films.

The Tower of London's complex history and enduring legends make it a fascinating subject for both historians and ghost enthusiasts. Whether viewed as a symbol of royal power or a haunted relic of the past, the Tower continues to captivate and inspire imaginations worldwide.

CHAPTER 21

THE TERRACOTTA ARMY

The Terracotta Army is one of the most remarkable archaeological discoveries of the 20th century, providing a vivid glimpse into the world of China's first emperor, Qin Shi Huang. This massive assembly of life-sized terracotta figures was created to accompany the emperor in his afterlife, reflecting his desire for immortality and showcasing his power and resources.

Posthumous depiction of Qin Shi Huang, 19th century

Qin Shi Huang ascended to the throne as the King of Qin at the age of 13 in 246 BCE. He quickly embarked on a series of conquests that would ultimately unify the warring states of China into a single empire by 221 BCE. Known for his ambitious projects, including the Great Wall of China, Qin Shi Huang also commissioned the construction of his grand mausoleum near Xi'an in Shaanxi Province, a project that would span nearly four decades and employ over 700,000 laborers.

The Terracotta Army was discovered in March 1974 by local farmers digging a well in Lintong County, near Xi'an. They stumbled upon a buried vault containing fragments of the terracotta figures. This accidental discovery led to extensive archaeological excavations revealing three main pits filled with over 8,000 soldiers, 130 chariots, and 670 horses.

The Terracotta Army figures were constructed using a form of mass production. Artisans crafted the bodies in an assembly-line fashion, molding different parts such as heads, arms, legs, and torsos separately before assembling them. Despite the standardized production, each figure was uniquely detailed with individualized facial features, hairstyles, and armor, giving the impression of a real army with diverse soldiers from various regions of China.

The figures were originally painted in vibrant colors, though much of the paint has faded over the centuries.

They were equipped with real weapons, many of which have been looted over time, but some of the surviving pieces, like bronze swords and crossbows, remain remarkably well-preserved.

Qin Shi Huang's mausoleum is a vast complex that remains largely unexcavated. Historical texts, particularly the "Records of the Grand Historian" by Sima Qian, describe an underground palace filled with precious arti-facts and a map of the emperor's empire with rivers of mercury representing water bodies. Modern scientific studies have indeed detected unusually high levels of mercury in the soil around the mausoleum, lending some credibility to these ancient accounts.

The Terracotta Army has also been shrouded in legends and claims of curses. Some believe that disturbing the tomb has brought bad luck to those involved. These claims are often fueled by the mysterious deaths and illnesses of several workers and archaeologists who first excavated the site. However, no scientific evidence supports the existence of a curse, and most of these claims remain in the realm of folklore.

Eyewitnesses and visitors to the Terracotta Army often describe a sense of awe and eeriness when viewing the silent, stoic figures. Some have reported feeling an inexplicable chill or hearing whispers among the rows of soldiers, though these experiences are subjective and not scientifically validated. The meticulous craftsmanship and the sheer scale of the army evoke a profound connection to the distant past, where the line between history and myth often blurs.

Today, the Terracotta Army is a major tourist attraction and a UNESCO World Heritage Site. The site includes a museum where visitors can view the pits containing the army and learn about the historical and cultural significance of this extraordinary find. Ongoing excavations continue to reveal new figures and artifacts, contributing to our understanding of ancient Chinese civilization.

The Chinese government has invested heavily in the preservation and protection of the site. Efforts include climate-controlled environments to prevent further deterioration of the figures and advanced archaeological techniques to uncover and restore additional parts of the mausoleum complex.

The Terracotta Army has captivated the imagination of people worldwide and has been featured in various forms of popular culture. It appears in movies, documentaries, and even video games, symbolizing the grandeur and mystery of ancient China. One notable reference is in the 2008 film "The Mummy: Tomb of the Dragon Emperor," where the Terracotta Army comes to life as part of the movie's plot.

The Terracotta Army stands as a testament to the ambition and legacy of Qin Shi Huang, reflecting both his achievements in unifying China and his profound obsession with immortality. As archaeological efforts continue, this silent army remains a powerful link to a bygone era, offering insights into the life and times of China's first emperor while continuing to inspire awe and wonder in all who behold it.

CHAPTER 22
POVEGLIA ISLAND

Poveglia Island, located in the Venetian Lagoon between Venice and Lido, has a history steeped in tragedy and death, earning it the grim title of one of the world's most haunted locations. The island first appeared in historical records in 421 AD when it served as a refuge from barbaric invasions. Over the centuries, it became a prosperous island with a growing population and strategic significance.

In the 14th century, Poveglia's dark legacy began during the outbreak of the bubonic plague, also known as the Black Death. Venice, a bustling hub of trade, was particularly vulnerable to the spread of the plague, which led to the establishment of quarantine stations known as lazarettos. Poveglia was transformed into one such station where those suspected of plague infection were isolated. The island became synonymous with death as thousands of infected individuals were sent there to die in isolation. Mass graves and pyres were used to dispose of the bodies, with reports suggesting that the soil of Poveglia is mixed with human ash.

The claims of hauntings on Poveglia Island have intrigued and terrified many, but there is no scientific evidence to support the supernatural activities reported by visitors. The psychological impact of the island's dark history, combined with its eerie and abandoned state, likely contributes to the sense of unease and the alleged paranormal experiences. The phenomenon of feeling cold spots, hearing disembodied voices, and seeing apparitions can often be attributed to the power of suggestion, the brain's response to fear, and environmental factors such as drafts and structural decay.

Numerous visitors and paranormal investigators have reported strange occurrences on Poveglia Island. These include hearing screams, moans, and whispers emanating from the decaying buildings. Some claim to have seen ghostly apparitions and felt physical touches or pushes from unseen forces. One of the most persistent legends involves the spirit of a doctor who allegedly conducted inhumane experiments on mental patients during the island's time as an asylum. According to the legend, this doctor was driven to madness by the tormented spirits and ultimately threw himself from the bell tower, his ghost said to haunt the island ever since.

In 1922, Poveglia's morbid history took another dark turn when a mental asylum was established on the island. Reports of cruel treatments and experimentation on patients quickly surfaced. Stories of lobotomies performed with rudimentary tools and other forms of torture became part of the island's lore. The asylum's director, allegedly a sadistic doctor, was said to have been tormented by the ghosts of his victims until he met a gruesome end by falling from the bell tower. This period added another layer of horror to Poveglia's already grue-some history.

Today, Poveglia Island remains abandoned and off-limits to the public due to safety concerns. Attempts to repurpose the island, such as transforming it into a luxury resort in the 1960s, have failed, largely due to its haunted reputation. In 2014, the Italian government auctioned a 99-year lease on the island in hopes of revitalizing it, but these plans have yet to come to fruition.

Poveglia's notoriety has made it a popular subject in pop culture, particularly within the paranormal and horror genres. The island has been featured in numerous documentaries and television shows, including episodes of "Ghost Adventures" and "Scariest Places on Earth," where paranormal investigators attempt to capture evidence of the supernatural. The island's haunted legacy continues to attract thrill-seekers and ghost hunters, despite the legal and physical barriers to visiting.

Poveglia Island's long history of death, disease, and suffering has undeniably left a mark on its identity, fostering countless tales of hauntings and curses. While scientific explanations can debunk many of the supernatural claims, the island's eerie atmosphere and tragic past continue to captivate the imagination of those intrigued by the macabre. Whether viewed as a historical site of immense human suffering or a haunted island teeming with restless spirits, Poveglia remains one of the most fascinating and terrifying places in the world.

CHAPTER 23

THE BUSBY STOOP CHAIR

The story of the Busby Stoop Chair begins with Thomas Busby, a notorious drunkard and petty criminal from North Yorkshire, England, in the late 17th century. Busby was married to Elizabeth, the daughter of Daniel Auty (sometimes spelled Awety), who was involved in counterfeiting and other illicit activities. The conflict between Busby and Auty reached a boiling point when Auty sat in Busby's favorite chair at the local inn, leading to a heated argument. That night, an enraged Busby followed Auty to his home and bludgeoned him to death with a hammer.

Busby was arrested, tried, and sentenced to death by hanging in 1702. On his way to the gallows, he cursed his chair, proclaiming that anyone who sat in it would die a gruesome death. The chair remained at the Busby Stoop Inn, named after the execution site, for centuries, becoming the centerpiece of many legends and alleged supernatural events.

The curse of the Busby Stoop Chair allegedly claimed its first victim in 1894, nearly 200 years after Busby's execution. A chimney sweep who sat in the chair was found dead the next morning, hanging from a post near the inn. Over the years, numerous other deaths were attributed to the chair. These included Canadian airmen during World War II, a roofer who fell to his death, a cleaning lady who died of a brain tumor shortly after sitting in the chair, and a delivery man who crashed his van after taking a seat in the infamous chair.

Eyewitness accounts from the 20th century further fueled the legend. For example, two RAF airmen reportedly sat in the chair and died in a car crash later that day.

A similar fate befell a group of builders, one of whom sat in the chair and later fell to his death from a roof.

Despite its eerie reputation, there is a scientific and skeptical perspective on the Busby Stoop Chair. Dr. Adam Bowett, a historian specializing in furniture, examined the chair and concluded that it was not from the 17th century. Instead, he found that the chair's spindles were machine-made, a technique not used until the 19th century, suggesting that the chair currently displayed is not the original cursed object.

Moreover, many deaths attributed to the chair can be explained through natural causes and coincidence. The high mortality rate of airmen during World War II, the inherently risky nature of jobs like roofing, and the general likelihood of accidents occurring in everyday life all contribute to the possibility that these incidents were not the result of a supernatural curse but rather unfortunate coincidences.

Eyewitness testimonies have played a significant role in maintaining the chair's legendary status. Visitors to the Thirsk Museum, where the chair is now displayed, have reported feelings of unease, chills, and even sightings of Busby's ghost near the chair. These subjective experiences, while compelling, lack empirical evidence and are often dismissed by skeptics as the power of suggestion and psychological priming.

The Busby Stoop Chair was finally removed from public use in 1978 after a series of fatal incidents. It now resides in the Thirsk Museum, mounted on the wall to prevent anyone from sitting in it. This measure aims to put an end to the chair's deadly reputation while still allowing it to be viewed as a historical and cultural artifact.

The chair has also made its way into popular culture, often featured in ghost hunting shows, paranormal documentaries, and folklore discussions. Its story has been retold in various media, keeping the legend alive in the public imagination.

The tale of the Busby Stoop Chair sits at the intersection of folklore and skepticism. While the numerous deaths associated with the chair are chilling, a rational examination suggests that many of these incidents could be attributed to coincidence, risky behavior, and psychological factors rather than a genuine curse. The discrepancy in the chair's age, as revealed by historical analysis, further complicates claims of its supernatural origins.

Ultimately, whether one believes in the curse or not, the Busby Stoop Chair remains a fascinating piece of history, encapsulating the enduring power of legends and the human propensity to find meaning in the unexplained.

CHAPTER 24
THE CATACOMBS OF PARIS

The Paris Catacombs, an extensive network of underground ossuaries, hold the remains of approximately six million people. The origins of this macabre site date back to the late 18th century when Paris faced a critical problem: overcrowded and unsanitary cemeteries posed serious public health risks. In 1780, the Cemetery of Innocents (Les Innocents), which had been in use for nearly a millennium, was closed due to these concerns. The decision to create the Catacombs emerged as a response to this crisis.

The Catacombs were established in the former lime-stone quarries beneath the city, which had been mined since the Roman era. These quarries, stretching for miles beneath Paris, provided a ready-made solution for the city's burial problems. The process of transferring remains from the city's cemeteries began in 1786, with bones being moved at night to avoid public outcry. The site was consecrated as the "Paris Municipal Ossuary" on April 7, 1786, and soon became known as the Catacombs, a reference to the Roman catacombs that had fascinated people since their discovery.

The Catacombs are not just a repository of bones; they are a testament to the ingenuity and artistic sensibilities of the period. The tunnels and chambers are meticulously organized, with bones arranged decoratively in patterns that blend functionality with aesthetics. Skulls and femurs are stacked in rows and columns, creating eerie yet symmetrical designs. Some sections even feature elaborate sculptures and arrangements that transform the space into a unique underground art gallery.

The Paris Catacombs have long been associated with ghost stories and tales of the supernatural. While there is no scientific evidence to support the existence of ghosts, several factors contribute to the eerie atmosphere that fuels these legends. The Catacombs are dark, damp, and labyrinthine, creating a sense of isolation and disorientation. The presence of human remains, combined with the dim lighting and narrow passages, can induce a psychological response in visitors, making them more susceptible to feelings of unease and fear.

Over the years, numerous visitors and explorers have reported strange experiences in the Catacombs. Some claim to have heard whispers and footsteps, seen shadowy figures, or felt sudden drops in temperature. One famous account involves an urban explorer named Philibert Aspairt, who disappeared in the Catacombs in 1793. His body was found 11 years later, and his tragic tale has become a part of the Catacombs' lore. Despite these stories, scientific explanations often point to the psychological impact of the environment and the power of suggestion.

Today, the Catacombs are one of Paris's most popular tourist attractions, drawing hundreds of thousands of visitors annually. Managed by the Carnavalet Museum, the Catacombs are open to the public, offering a fascinating yet somber glimpse into the city's history. Visitors can explore about 1.5 kilometers of the ossuary, a small fraction of the vast network that lies beneath Paris.

Modern renovations have improved accessibility, and guided tours provide historical context and safety for visitors. The experience is both educational and reflective, offering insights into the challenges of urban management in historical Paris and the cultural attitudes towards death and remembrance.

The Catacombs have permeated popular culture, inspiring numerous works of fiction, films, and art. They have appeared in novels such as Victor Hugo's *Les Misérables* and Gaston Leroux's *The Phantom of the Opera*. More recently, the Catacombs were featured in the 2014 horror film *As Above, So Below*, which capitalizes on the site's creepy and claustrophobic environment to create a sense of dread and suspense.

The Paris Catacombs stand as a symbol of the city's rich and tumultuous history. From their origins as a solution to a public health crisis to their current status as a major tourist attraction, the Catacombs continue to captivate and intrigue. Whether one visits for the history, the art, or the thrill of the macabre, the Catacombs offer a unique journey into the depths of Paris's past and a reminder of the ever-present specter of mortality.

❧

If you enjoyed this book, pick up another exciting book by bestselling author Ethan Hayes.

ABOUT THE AUTHOR

Ethan Hayes grew up in Oklahoma and moved to Texas when he attended Texas A&M. Upon graduation he was hired by Texas Parks and Wildlife and remained there until he retired twenty-two years later. He currently lives in southeast Texas with his wife and two dogs. When he's not spending time enjoying the outdoors and writing, he sips a cold beer on his front porch while listening to Bluegrass music.

☙❧

Send in your encounter story:
encountersbigfoot@gmail.com

ALSO BY ETHAN HAYES

ENCOUNTERS IN THE WOODS

WHAT LURKS BEYOND

FEAR IN THE FOREST

INTO THE DARKNESS

ENCOUNTERS BIGFOOT

TALES OF TERROR

I SAW BIGFOOT

STALKED: TERRIFYING TRUE CRIME STORIES

CONSPIRACY THEORIES THAT WERE TRUE

THE BIG BIGFOOT BOOK SERIES

THE MEGA MONSTER BOOK SERIES

ALSO BY FREE REIGN PUBLISHING

www.ingramcontent.com/pod-product-compliance
Lightning Source LLC
Chambersburg PA
CBHW032111280326
41933CB00009B/796